What p...

God, who ...

This is a gem of a book, one of profound honesty in the search for the 'Other'; it tracks the astonished discovery that a life given over to following the path of Christ can actually make sense. At every point it is helpfully challenging, unafraid to contemplate the difficulties of Christianity, and willing to demonstrate how Christian belief can make the world a better place. Human beings are now looking to learn how to give expression to our post-Covid thirst for hope and meaning; and this is the very book for them

Nicholas King SJ, Assistant Catholic Chaplain at Oxford University

Stephen has written an engaging book weaving together theological exploration with spiritual journeying and autobiographical reflection. His style is clear and jargon-free, and he has clearly ranged freely and widely in his reading and thinking, presenting a version of the Christian faith which reflects his vigorously progressive Catholicism. I love his emphasis on living with the mystery of God, and found his reflections on his own spiritual journey, especially the importance of pilgrimage, to resonate profoundly. This book will take its place within the genre of accessible Christian apologetic, and will play its part in engaging with those on the fringes of faith who will be attracted to a lively and attractive presentation of the Christian faith which begins with the wonder and mystery of God and his creation. In his own pilgrimage of faith and his vision of hope for humanity he is a twenty-first-century Gerard Hughes.

David Meara, Archdeacon Emeritus of London

As an Anglican medical scientist, I was delighted to find myself in sympathy and agreement with most of the views of the author, a deeply Catholic, physics-trained economist. Stephen McCarthy presents a very intelligent and readable discussion of the many questions that beset and intrigue those of us who try to make coherent sense of the place of religious conviction in our present world, and how those convictions should guide our actions in the growing crises which affect us all.
Dr John Morris, Emeritus Fellow in medicine of St Hugh's College, Oxford

Stephen McCarthy's short book is timely. Most church congregations are in decline and people appear increasingly inclined to look elsewhere for meaning, and purpose, in life. I found the book perceptive and challenging. I commend it to anyone interested in living a truly fulfilled life or playing a part – however small – in making this a better world.
Jackie Jones, Ordained Church of England priest and Hospice Chaplain

Previous books by the author
The Political Economy of Botswana: A Study of Growth and Distribution
(Oxford, OUP, 1980) (With Christopher Colclough) ISBN 0198771363

Africa: the challenge of transformation (London, Tauris, 1994). ISBN 1850438218

Edited: *The Contagion of Jesus: Doing Theology as if it Mattered* by Sebastian Moore (London, Darton, Longman & Todd, 2007). ISBN 9780232527179

God, who on Earth are You?

Mystery and Meaning
in Christianity today

God, who on Earth are You?

Mystery and Meaning in Christianity today

Stephen McCarthy

CHRISTIAN ALTERNATIVE
BOOKS

Winchester, UK
Washington, USA

JOHN HUNT PUBLISHING

First published by Christian Alternative Books, 2022
Christian Alternative Books is an imprint of John Hunt Publishing Ltd.,
No. 3 East St., Alresford, Hampshire SO24 9EE, UK
office@jhpbooks.com
www.johnhuntpublishing.com
www.christian-alternative.com

For distributor details and how to order please visit the 'Ordering' section on our website.

ISBN: 978 1 78904 943 5
978 1 78904 944 2 (ebook)
Library of Congress Control Number: 2021939191

A CIP catalogue record for this book is available from the British Library.

Design: Stuart Davies

UK: Printed and bound by CPI Group (UK) Ltd, Croydon, CR0 4YY
Printed in North America by CPI GPS partners

We operate a distinctive and ethical publishing philosophy in
all areas of our business, from our global network of authors to
production and worldwide distribution.

Contents

Preface

This book seemed to come from nowhere. One day, during the first 2020 lockdown, I opened my laptop and started to type. Now that I come to introduce it to you who will read it, I see that – like most writing – it is composed of the different threads of my own experience. The first thread – perhaps the warp – is the Roman Catholic Church. I was born and brought up in a Catholic family in the UK. God was very much present in our lives, but a rather shadowy figure, more fearsome than loving. God, through his mouthpiece – the Catholic Church – had set out precise, unchanging rules for us (the faithful) to follow (not least concerning sexual morality), and woe betide any deviation from them. Since then the Church has changed, and become much more open to the world, which has also changed almost beyond recognition from how we experienced it fifty years ago. And I, also, have changed as a result of the experiences of a lifetime – which I outline in more detail in the Introduction. All these form the weft of this text. They seemed to me to be connected and these I wanted to explore and weave together.

I do not know why you have picked up this book. Are you a member of the Church, discontented with the direction organised religion is taking, or concerned at the slow pace of change, worried that the pews are empty, or wondering why God seems irrelevant to too many of our fellow citizens' lives? Perhaps you are one of those people who feels the tug of something you can give no name to in your life, you might be someone who has walked a pilgrim path, or is sustained by silent thought or a meditative practice. Or you may be actively involved in any of the multitude of ways that concerned people try to bring about change in the world. I hope I have something to say to all such readers, and may even suggest connections that help you find some meaning in life and to make sense of questions we all need to resolve for ourselves if we are to see our way.

I begin at the beginning – by plunging into the deep and mysterious waters of what Christianity believes and what God really is (chapters 1 and 2) and then turn to God's Creation and how this belief complements but does not contradict our scientific understanding of the world (chapter 3). Although God and his creative power are unfathomable, we are nevertheless invited into a personal relationship with God, which I explore in the three chapters of Part II – on Prayer, Pilgrimage and Spirituality (chapters 4, 5 and 6). But a 'me and my God' spirituality is not sufficient; it has to be sustained and deepened by community. We humans live in community and need community in order to be fully alive – many of us experienced the loss of community closely during the period in 2020 and 2021 when we were 'locked down' and cut off from normal human relations. The Christian Churches are human institutions that offer this community. But as with all human institutions, they can be deeply flawed and need to be reformed and rebuilt: this is the topic of chapters 7 and 8 (Part III). Finally, the Christian calling is a calling not only to relationship with God but also to cooperation with God in renewing the earth and human society. What this might mean in the time and place in which we live is tentatively discussed in the closing chapters of this book. So Part IV asks what Christianity, and individual Christians, are called to do to live out the life of Jesus in the world today.

This short text will appear quite hard-hitting and indeed controversial in many places. Many people hoped that our world would change for the better after the 2020/21 pandemic was over. But I do not speculate on this. I wanted to write a text that was not too attached to a particular moment in history, though of course we are all greatly influenced by the time, customs and culture in which we live. Nevertheless, my conviction, deeply held, is that there is hope for the world. God continues his slow work of redemption, in which we are invited to cooperate in our own small and diverse ways. One thing we can be sure of: the future will not turn out as we expect.

Many people have supported me during the writing of this text. As I shut myself away, bent over my computer, my wife, Carol, had to put up with even greater social isolation than the pandemic itself required. She also made wise, timely suggestions, at various points in its preparation. Others who have contributed helpfully by reading and commenting on successive drafts include: my sister Marian, Marcella Creed, Julia Knowles, Margaret and David Broadhurst, Ewa Bem and Aleksandra Trzcinska. But I am quite sure that the book would never have been finished without the input and active encouragement of Rosemary Roberts at every stage. Her detailed suggestions and proposed improvements to the text, including correcting factual errors and improving the style and punctuation, have certainly enhanced its content and clarity. Indeed, some of the more lyrical passages in the text bear the mark of her pen. But, of course, I alone take responsibility for the mistakes, fallacies and ambiguities that remain.

Introduction

As a young child my ambition for when I grew up was to be a hermit. This was probably a consequence of reading too many pious and indeed fantastical lives of the saints written for children. Fortunately I have never achieved this ambition, though my wife still detects the same dormant inclination. But life has since taught me that we are only fully human when we are in community with others. Besides, I think that in practice hermits are often besieged by visitors seeking their advice and wisdom. Then, from the age of 7, I was fortunate enough to be educated by the Jesuits (the Society of Jesus). It is often said that if you give the Jesuits a 7-year-old they will 'give you the man'. In my case this is true, as will become clear, so Ignatian spirituality – that followed by the Jesuits – is a strong thread in this story! The Jesuits are indeed an extraordinary, and historically controversial, group of men, often very talented in diverse ways and sometimes quite eccentric. They are reputed to live under strict orders and discipline from their superiors. But the reality is quite different. Each is encouraged to 'discern' (a very Jesuit word) his own particular vocation and to grow and develop accordingly. The result is a huge variety of opinions, including theological opinions, and ways of living life within the Society – but still some common *esprit du corps*. So in these pages you will meet the remarkable Jesuit Gerard Hughes who, among other things, taught me the little German I know. It was said that he had taught himself German in order to read Goethe in the original. He later wrote *God of Surprises*, a spiritual book that has sold a quarter of a million copies around the world in several different languages.[1] Gerard Hughes, along with Michael Ivens, another Jesuit you will meet later, whom I also knew in my schooldays, established the well-known St Beuno's Spirituality Centre in north Wales. One of the schoolboy stories that circulated about Michael was that he always slept in an armchair, as he was simply too disorganised to bother going to bed. More personally, I recall his solicitous care for me at a Scout camp in *la France profonde*, when I was racked by diarrhoea. I got to know him again towards the end of his life, by which time he was suffering from a brain tumour. I remember at one meeting he discussed the choice he had to make as to whether or not to have an operation that would certainly leave him blind but would probably prolong his life for a few years. The next time I met him he was blind.

On leaving school, I studied physics at Oxford. By this time my parents, who had always been committed Catholics, loyal to the Church, were becoming increasingly critical of it as a human institution. In this respect I tended to follow in their footsteps. For a term, I was president of the Newman Society in Oxford (the University Catholic Society), and in that capacity I invited Charles Davis in May 1967 to speak at the University Catholic Chaplaincy. Davis was a very eminent English Catholic theologian, who had rather angrily and publicly left the Catholic Church the December before, arguing that it was too authoritarian (an opinion that seemed justified, at least for that time). Cardinal Heenan, then Archbishop of Westminster, heard of this invitation and wrote threateningly to the University Catholic Chaplain, the saintly Michael Hollings – another priest who was said to sleep regularly in an armchair, and frequently took in homeless people. It was typical of the Catholic hierarchy that Heenan did not have the courtesy to write to me, who, as president of the society, had actually issued the invitation. We wished to avoid getting Hollings into trouble, but did not want to disinvite Davis, so we switched the meeting venue to the premises of the Student Christian Movement, who were very happy to oblige.

Even before I had finished my degree, my interest in physics had been replaced by a concern for the development of the

'Third World', as it was called in those days. Where this interest came from, I do not now remember. Certainly, Jesus' concern for the poor and the marginalised is perhaps the strongest theme in his teaching, as passed down to us in the Gospels, but I cannot say that I recall any direct carry-over from my Christian faith into this new interest in my life – though the connection has certainly become clearer in more recent years. I soon discovered that if I wanted a career in 'development' the lack of a degree in economics was a distinct disadvantage. Nevertheless, through determination on my part, together with a sequence of seemingly random coincidences – or, as I might say now, because I was drawn in the right direction – I ended up three years later in an economic planning post in the Ministry of Finance and Development Planning in Botswana.

To work in Botswana in the early 1970s was an amazing experience. The government of Sir Seretse Khama was democratic, pragmatic and incorrupt. That he was both the elected president but also the traditional 'chief' of the largest tribal grouping in the country certainly helped. With the recent discovery of diamonds, the economy was growing at around 15% a year. Botswana may now be somewhat less democratic and incorrupt, and its economy is less dynamic than it was, but the country remains a striking example of probity and progress on the African continent. I met my wife, Carol, in Botswana, and in 1976 Julian Black, a missionary priest there, married us in his little mud-walled, thatched-roof church in the village of Thamaga, where he had also established a small successful pottery for the villagers to earn some income through learning and practising a new skill. He, too, will appear again later in these pages.

After nearly six years in Botswana, we returned to England in 1977. I had no job, was ill with hepatitis (not contracted in Botswana), and our first child was about to be born. Again, a series of unlikely connections led to my recruitment by the European Investment Bank (an institution of the EU) in Luxembourg. I was hired to work as a development economist on the EU development assistance programme in anglophone Africa, as well as the small island nations of the Caribbean and Pacific. This assistance programme was a new initiative at the time, following the UK's accession to the EU. During this period, I visited, at one time or another, nearly half of the countries in sub-Saharan Africa, as well as many of those in the Caribbean and Pacific. But I was puzzled that there was so little real 'development' in almost all of them, in stark contrast with my experience in Botswana. In due course, my employer graciously offered me a sabbatical, and I returned to Oxford to study the question and eventually to write a book on the matter.[2] One of my principal conclusions was that aid programmes, not just those of the EU, were largely paternalistic and ineffective. Rather, ordinary people know better than outsiders what will improve their lives and how to organise themselves. So aid agencies should provide cash incomes to poor people and this, together with primary education, especially for girls, would eventually be more effective than most current aid programmes. These conclusions have stayed with me ever since, and certainly influence the later chapters of this book.

In 2005, after twenty-seven years and at the age of 58, my professional career was stalled, so I took the opportunity of early retirement from the EIB. In the meantime, I had noticed in myself a growing interest in spirituality. Despite the practice of my faith having become somewhat routine during this long period of my life, I had started making annual religious retreats, in the Jesuit tradition of St Ignatius – in effect returning to the influences of my education. So, after my retirement, I decided to follow the Spiritual Exercises of St Ignatius, which consist of a thirty-day silent meditative retreat programme. This takes you deep into yourself before bringing you back to the world around you. (We will revisit the Spiritual Exercises later in the book.) In fact I followed a three-month programme, which offered more opportunity to reflect on and draw lessons from the experience. Some time later, I trained as a spiritual director myself, in Belgium, under the guidance of Franck Janin, another eminent and wise Jesuit.

At one point during the Spiritual Exercises, my 'director' introduced me to the work of Sebastian Moore, who had published a number of short, rather disorganised, controversial but very insightful theological books. Shortly afterwards, my father handed me a bundle of papers, which he said were a collection of Sebastian's unpublished essays and sermons; he thought they would probably be of more interest to me than they were to him. (Many years earlier, in the late 1960s, my parents and others had collaborated with Sebastian on a campaign to change the teaching of the Catholic Church on birth control.)[3] These unpublished papers seemed to be worth offering to readers, so I contacted Sebastian, who was by then nearly 90, about doing so. He was still actively writing, both prose and poems. Indeed, he told me that some mornings the first thing he did on waking up was to write a sonnet. So, I compiled and edited a selection of Sebastian's new material. The book, *The Contagion of Jesus: Doing Theology as if it Mattered*, appeared in 2007 and was short-listed for the Michael Ramsey Theological Prize in 2009.[4] As a result of this collaboration my understanding of many Christian doctrines, such as the humanity of Jesus and the meaning of his Crucifixion and Resurrection, deepened – or rather, I became more deeply drawn into the mysterious nature of all this teaching, as you will see in the following pages.

In 2006 I started walking the Camino de Santiago in France and Spain – pilgrims and pilgrimage form another important thread here. I covered about a thousand miles in stages with a group of friends over a period of several years. As a consequence of that pilgrimage experience, in 2014 my wife and I set up a shelter for pilgrims on the Camino de Santiago. In talking with them, and listening to them, I realised how many people were still searching for the 'Other' – for God, if you like – but how often they had rejected the Church, despite walking along an ancient Christian pilgrimage route. I learned much from them as they talked about their disillusionments, but also about their hopes for the future.

At the same time, at least partly because of the international first-hand experience I had had during my working life, I was becoming increasingly concerned with the scandals of social injustice and wealth disparity in our world, as well as with the overshadowing, and closely related, issue of environmental destruction. I am convinced that politics and faith are inseparable, in that both are concerned with shaping the society in which we want to live, and that as Christians we should not be complacent and passive but rather, in cooperation with others of all religions and none, should do what we can to bring about a different future.

So here are the motifs that run through this book and are developed in it: God and Jesus, the spirituality of St Ignatius, pilgrimage, the Church, the family of humankind and what the Christian faith teaches us about inequity, injustice and the needs of the world in the context of environmental degradation. That these far-reaching and serious matters are connected, and that they are of vital importance to every human person are, to my mind, beyond dispute.

A couple of clarifications

Before we go on, it seems important to define two terms: 'the Church' and 'the Bible'. About both of these I make assumptions that it would be unfair on you, the reader, not to explain. By 'the Church' I mean, the collective unity of all the Christian Churches taken together. Much of the time my focus is on the (Roman) Catholic Church, which is still by far the most numerous and geographically diverse of the various Christian Churches, and I usually make clear that I am doing so. However, many of my comments will also apply to other Christian Churches or denominations, sometimes explicitly named. But I have no personal experience of the Orthodox Church, the Pentecostal Churches or the mega-Churches that have grown so rapidly in some corners of the world, so my comments may not be appropriate to them. I consider Churches that interpret the Bible literally and uncritically to have left the mainstream of the Christian tradition: they should be understood to be excluded from general references, as I cannot speak for them.

To explain that last point: the Bible is not a book. It is a hugely diverse library of books – stories – chosen and put together in a particular (not always logical) order over time. Each one reveals something of who or what God is and of God's relations with humankind. The Old Testament books are the Jewish scriptures and tell the ancient stories of the Jewish people. The New Testament books take up the story, from Jesus' birth to the beginnings of the early Church, and, together with the Old Testament, make up the body of Christian scripture. There is other early writing about Jesus Christ, which was excluded from the agreed New Testament when the selection was made in the fourth century. These excluded texts are sometimes referred to as the Gnostic or apocryphal Gospels.

All the books of the Bible are essentially stories, written by different authors, and sometimes they seem to contradict one another, especially when they tell different versions of the same story. This is exactly how *we* tell stories. I often find, when my wife is telling the story of some incident in our life, that I want to interrupt and say: 'No, that isn't how it was at all.' But it is what the story tells us that is important, not the exact details, and sometimes the same story can be told in different ways to bring out different aspects. So it is with Bible stories. It stands to reason, therefore, that a literal interpretation of the Bible is logically unsustainable in the light of what we know about human authorship, no matter how deeply inspired by God.

In reality it is possible to find something in the Bible that could justify almost any opinion, and this is what some more 'evangelical' Christian denominations do. But the mainstream Churches, the Catholic Church in particular, consider that the selection of relevant biblical stories has to be influenced by 'tradition', the accumulated wisdom of Christianity, as interpreted by some form of 'teaching authority'. The net result of course is that these Churches *also* tend to pick and choose their biblical stories. For example, the final book of 'Revelation' is largely, though certainly not completely, ignored in Catholic religious services. The danger, of course, is that in the end what the 'teaching authority' has to say may seem to overwhelm the essential message of Jesus – as seemed to be the case in my childhood. This too is a theme that will run through the later chapters of this book.

Finally, my biblical quotations are taken from the *New Revised Standard Version* of the Bible. This is a widely accepted scholarly text, but it does not necessarily adopt the most colloquial language nor does it strive to be gender neutral. God is personal but does not have gender. Yet I have adopted the male pronoun for God as this has been the most commonly used in the past and none of the alternatives so far proposed seems satisfactory. I apologise to those who find this offensive. I will come to the Christian doctrine of the Trinity in chapter 2, but let me say that we think first of God the Father – the Creator – then God the Son – the Redeemer – who took human form in the male person of Jesus Christ and third God the Holy Spirit – considered to be the giver of life. Life-giving feels a particularly feminine gift so I personally think of the Holy Spirit as female and will use the feminine pronoun whenever she is specifically mentioned.

1   Gerard W. Hughes, *God of Surprises* (London: Darton, Longman & Todd, 1985)

2   Stephen McCarthy, *Africa: the challenge of transformation* (London, Tauris, 1984)

3   Pope Paul VI's 'encyclical' letter (a formal teaching document written by the pope) entitled *Humanae vitae* ('On human life'), published in 1968, reasserted the traditional Catholic teaching on artificial birth control – namely, that it was always wrong. This was directly contrary to the conclusion of the Pontifical Commission on Birth Control, which the Pope had himself set up precisely to re-examine the issue. Since then, many educated and thinking Catholics have made up their own minds and simply ignore the encyclical.

4   Sebastian Moore, *The Contagion of Jesus: Doing Theology as if it Mattered* (London, Darton, Longman & Todd, 2007)

Part I: Who Is God?

Faith is not a commodity
To be possessed,
A bargaining counter
Used to get things done;
Faith is the orientation
Of our lives, a gift
Which shifts perceptions,
Takes us deeper
Into the mystery of God.[1]

* * *

We start by exploring the mystery of what people of the Christian faith believe God to be, and how the whole life and teaching of Jesus point us towards the depths of that mystery. We shall also touch briefly on how our deepening human knowledge, through science and philosophy, may elucidate some small aspects of that belief, even as the utter reality of God remains beyond our comprehension – at least on this side of the grave.

1   Ann Lewin, *Watching for the Kingfisher: poems and prayers* (London: Canterbury Press, 2009), p. 5

1 The Christian Story

Christianity is one of the world's great religions – along with Buddhism, Hinduism, Islam and Judaism. All of them point to some transcendence beyond ourselves that we can never fully grasp or understand, and which is usually called God. All offer pathways towards the mystery of this presence. And the further you walk along one of these paths, the more the inessentials and accretions – the special language, imagery and forms – of the religion you are following fall away, as you are drawn towards an elusive destination, where you find yourself meeting those who have arrived by another route.

What, then, is the unique claim of Christianity? It is simply that the Creator God is actually so in love with his Creation and with humanity that he chose, at a certain point in history, to become part of that Creation in the form of the human person Jesus Christ – an event that we call the Incarnation. No other religion makes such a bold and, indeed, *incredible* – unbelievable – claim. Jesus is thus the central figure of the Christian story. When he said: 'I am the Way, the Truth and the Life' (John 14:6), he was saying that by following him and being like him we can find our way to God, discover the truth about God and live with God. Jesus did not just preach about God; his whole life was a kind of window – the best window we have – for us to perceive, to the limit of our understanding, who or what God is.[1]

Christianity certainly acknowledges that God is present in other religions – in so far as love and compassion lie at the centre of their teaching – and also to those who adhere to no religion at all. It teaches that God loves and reaches out to everyone without exception, whether they are Christian or not. And most Christian Churches – including the Catholic Church, especially over the last sixty years since the Second Vatican Council (Vatican II)[2] – are respectful of other religions and explicitly acknowledge that there may be things to learn and understand by drawing on the traditions and teachings of other faiths. Indeed, Pope Francis – the head of the Catholic Church – seems to go out of his way to draw other religions into his ambit. Nevertheless, if you stand inside the Christian faith, Christianity is not just *one* of the great religions: it is simply *the* principal story of God's relationship with humanity, though other religions – Islam in particular – contest this and make a similar claim for themselves.

The shock of Jesus

Jesus' teaching on earth was so radical, controversial and threatening to the religious authorities of his time and place that he was murdered by crucifixion. But on the third day after his death, by an incomprehensible and seismic intervention of God, he was restored to life again, not as a ghost, but in some bodily form that we do not understand. In short, Christianity teaches that Jesus' Incarnation, Crucifixion and Resurrection taken together comprise the most important event in human history.

By now, many of us are so completely used to this story that it no longer astounds us. It is, after all, the background to Western civilisation. But in truth, if we really did believe and strive to comprehend it, we would certainly live our lives in a very different manner. Jesus' disciples and apostles were so overwhelmed by this experience that they were completely changed, and, after his departure from the world, set out with enormous courage and energy, of a kind they had never shown before, to proclaim this news to everyone around them – as is depicted in the New Testament book of the Acts of the Apostles.

This new understanding of God's relationship with humanity spread like wildfire, despite the efforts of the Roman and some Jewish authorities to suppress it, and indeed to persecute the early Christians. Paul was one of the persecutors, until his dramatic conversion on the road to Damascus (Acts 9:1–22).[3] Subsequently in his Epistles (letters) to the early emerging Christian communities, which were scattered around the Middle East, Paul laboured to understand and explain the meaning of Jesus' life. He travelled constantly, encouraging and supporting the first Christians, while declaring that, with Jesus' death and Resurrection, everything had changed completely. The work of trying to interpret and share the mystery of Jesus' teaching has continued ever since, though rarely smoothly, and always controversially.

It seems impossible for us now to capture that early astonishment, and even bewilderment, but I have always loved a short passage, attributed to the Swedish church historian Bengt Sundkler as he describes the coming of Christianity to sub-Saharan Africa many centuries later. The young men leave their villages and go off to the new towns and settlements of the colonial power:

> The theme in all these cases is the same: groups of young men looking for a job in order to buy the best that money could give, a musket of one's own or a new rifle, and in the process finding a new religion. And then the triumphant return home, the people of the village congregate to welcome their intrepid young men. They lift their guns to shoot, and thus to punctuate their travel story. But in the evening they will gather their contemporaries, and show them their greatest treasure: a book, a Gospel of S. Matthew, or perhaps even a New Testament, and they can read from it.[4]

What is it about Jesus' teaching that appeals so strongly to those who come upon it for the first time? I suggest three key elements. First, Jesus (following the revelation of God in the Hebrew scriptures) taught that there is just one God, not the many gods of earlier belief systems, and that this one God is not merely a more powerful god in a divine hierarchy, lording it over other lesser deities, but is rather the *only* God. Second, Jesus not only preached, but also demonstrated, that – unlike the many dangerous and capricious deities and spirits of the pagan world, who had to be appeased – this God personally loves and longs to be loved by each one of us, and does not punish us for offending him. Third, he underlined again and again that, regardless of our status in the world, every person is created in God's own image and has equal value in God's eyes. The occasion in my life when this third aspect struck me most forcefully was at an early morning Mass in Tanzania, when I found myself kneeling at the communion rail next to a poor, bare-foot peasant. I can still see in my mind's eye the lined, leathery soles of his feet.

A roadside crucifix in France

The stories about Jesus and his teaching that have come down to us first circulated among his followers by word of mouth, and began to be written down only several decades after his death, at which point they were codified into a collection of books, prayers and doctrines. We shall discuss some of these in subsequent pages. But at this point I want merely to draw attention to another extraordinary fact about Christianity. It has chosen as its central image, its main symbol, a ghastly depiction of a man being tortured to death on a cross. Again, the very familiarity of this image has inured us to the reality of what it shows. But, aside from its horror, it encapsulates some key aspects of Christ's teaching: first, that it is essentially radical and can lead to persecution and death for believers; second, that God, in the person of Jesus Christ, was himself willing to undergo torture and death and, in that sense, be in solidarity with all those who suffer in the world. Christ did not promise a life free of hardship, grief and suffering, but rather promised to be with us on the journey through life.[5] Why a God who loves each one of us unconditionally should allow us, or indeed anyone at all, to suffer is mysterious. Millions of words have been written trying to explain this, but in the end no explanation is satisfactorily convincing.

Christianity teaches that Jesus had both a human and a divine nature, that he was both God and man. This is one of the many impenetrable mysteries within the Christian faith. I think most Christians tend to focus on Jesus' divinity, to the neglect of his existence as a fully human person. I certainly used to do so myself. But the writing of Sebastian Moore encouraged me to think harder about this. I rather think now that, like all human beings, Jesus, in his humanity, had slowly to discover what it was that he was called to do. Certainly, he must always have had an awareness of his immense closeness to God the Father, whom he addressed as his Abba, a term of great affection something like his 'Daddy'. But he spent the first thirty years of his life in rural obscurity. Then his public life begins with his baptism by John the Baptist, after which a voice from 'heaven' proclaims: 'This is my Son, the Beloved, with whom I am well pleased' (Matthew 3:17). So, is this perhaps the beginning of Jesus' discovery of his true purpose? Immediately after this, he retires to the desert for forty days of prayer and reflection, at the end of which he appears to know what he is called to do and how to do it – as illustrated through the recounting of a series of temptations by 'Satan'. Then he starts to gather his disciples. Yet, even later in his life, other people actually seem to help him to see his mission more clearly – not least the bold Canaanite woman, whom Jesus initially declines to help on the grounds that she is not 'of the house of Israel', but who rebukes him saying that even the dogs under the table get the scraps – upon which he relents (Matthew 15:22–28).

I need to be clear in what I am saying here. Ever since the Council of Chalcedon, in AD 451 – indeed, even long before that

– the Church has consistently proclaimed that Jesus was *both* human and divine. This belief is crucial to a second mystery that Sebastian grappled with: an explanation of Jesus' Crucifixion. Christian teaching frequently talks of this as a 'sacrifice' to save us all from our sins or to 'pay the price for our sins'. Whatever this means exactly, this idea certainly depends on a belief in Jesus' *divinity*; saving the world from its sins could not come about by any merely human action. Sometime there is an additional implication that this sacrifice was necessary in order to *appease* God the Father on our behalf. But God loves us and does not need sacrifice. As Hosea, one of the prophets of the Old Testament, says explicitly, in the voice of God: 'I desire steadfast love and not sacrifice, the knowledge of God rather than burnt offerings' (Hosea 6:6). This idea of Jesus appeasing God the Father arises from a false image of God as demanding, even vengeful. It is a projection onto God of some of the worst aspects of human behaviour. So this explanation of appeasing God is definitely to be rejected.

At the other extreme we might explain the Crucifixion in political terms; that the secular and religious authorities of his time simply had to get rid of a troublemaker. This is true, but the real meaning of the Crucifixion lies deeper than this. What is important may be that his death was not *demanded* by a vengeful God, but was entered into voluntarily by Jesus. But this still doesn't explain why Jesus' Crucifixion was *necessary*, or why the idea of 'sacrifice' seems so important in our understanding of it. It may be something like the sacrifice of his life that a mountain rescue worker makes in trying to save a climber trapped on a mountainside. Or perhaps it is akin to the sacrifices made by many women and men slaughtered by so-called 'security forces' as they try to oppose an evil political regime. For these people, their 'sacrifice' is something they are driven to do out of love; they feel they have no alternative. It may also be helpful to think of the 'sins' from which we are saved, not only as individual sins, but as the broken, unjust, exploitative societies that humanity makes for itself and which Jesus' teaching promises to overcome. Yet the full meaning of the Crucifixion remains mysterious – to me, at least. Still, I find an incomplete, but sufficient, explanation of Jesus' Crucifixion is that the whole story of his Incarnation, Crucifixion and Resurrection is simply God's purely gratuitous way of showing to humanity what God really is: unconditional love and 'compassion' – a word that means 'suffering with'. God, to make himself known to humanity, takes on human form in the fully human person of Jesus Christ, who speaks truth to power, is murdered for doing so, and then triumphantly overcomes death three days later.

The Resurrection story is of course equally mysterious and incomprehensible. The Church teaches that the risen Jesus was not some sort of ghost but rather a real bodily person. The evidence for this is that the tomb itself was empty and that after his Resurrection Jesus invited the apostle Thomas to touch his hands and side (John 20:24–27); he also ate and drank. One of my favourite passages in all the New Testament is the story, right at the end of John's Gospel, of Jesus engaged in the mundane task of cooking breakfast for his disciples on the shore of the Sea of Tiberias (John 21:1–14). Yet the risen Jesus did not seem to be constrained by limits of time and space, appearing when and where he wished. Ultimately, the most convincing explanation of the reality of the Resurrection was the impact it had on Jesus' disciples and apostles, as they were transformed from frightened and dejected people after the Crucifixion into an enthusiastic and determined group anxious to pass on the teaching they had heard from Jesus to other people. This change of heart was further strengthened on the occasion of Pentecost, fifty days later, when, as the Church teaches, they were 'confirmed' or strengthened by the Holy Spirit.

Importantly, the Church also teaches that death is certainly not the end for us; rather, that at the end of 'time' – whatever that means, as we shall discuss in chapter 3 – we too will be 'resurrected', though how and in what form we do not know. This is a message of deep hope for us all, particularly at those moments of grief when our loved ones pass away.

These few paragraphs summarise the only things about which I am reasonably certain. Yet they are also utterly mysterious. The Christian story is an invitation to enter into and taste these mysteries even if they are often proclaimed by the Church with apparent certainty in language and rituals that have lost their real meaning. My hope is that, as you read on, you will find yourself opening up to these mysteries and indeed to many other unanswered questions and speculations, both about Christianity itself and about the unfathomable nature of the world – God's Creation. Yet from the depths of these mysteries we can discover profound and counter-intuitive lessons of how to live our present lives in the community, society and age in which we live – as will emerge in the later chapters of this book.

1 In scripture and in Church teaching, Jesus, the Son of God, is frequently called the *Word*. Everything about him and his life is an image, a teaching, of what God is really like. See for example: (John 1:1–5, 14).

2 Vatican II was a major Council of the Catholic Church, held in Rome from 1962 to 1965. It reviewed and renewed much of that Church's teaching.

3 Paul is sometimes referred to as an apostle, though he did not know Jesus personally and was not one of the apostles originally chosen by Jesus.

4 Quoted in R. Oliver, *The African Experience* (London: Weidenfeld and Nicolson, 1991), p. 205.

5 Some offshoots of Christianity teach what is known as the 'prosperity Gospel': that if we are 'good' God will reward us with prosperity and good fortune in this life. This is an attractive idea but is fundamentally wrong.

2 A Mysterious God

Our image of God

When people say to me: 'Do you really believe in God?' I sometimes reply: 'I don't believe in the God you don't believe in.' The word 'God' conveys such a range of images in people's minds that it would perhaps be better if we stopped using the word at all, and instead said something like the 'Transcendent'.

When, in my capacity as a spiritual director,[1] I find myself at the beginning of a journey of spiritual accompaniment with another person, the first question to explore is the image of God that the person holds. Gerard W. Hughes, in his hugely successful book *God of Surprises*, discusses this at some length.[2] He concludes from his experience that many people, perhaps particularly those who as children were brought up in a Christian denomination, have an image of God as 'Good Old Uncle George', much admired by their parents but who is in fact 'gruff and threatening' and lives in a formidable mansion with a blazing furnace in the cellar, where those 'men, women and children who failed to visit Uncle George or to act in a way he approved' are sent. Certainly, this recalls my own image of God as a child. No wonder people, as they mature and let go of childish notions, reject such a God and, in the absence of any continuing spiritual growth or religious education, fail to find an acceptable alternative.

Christianity's understanding of God comes out of the pre-Christian Jewish tradition. Unlike most other tribes and peoples in pre-Christian times, the people of Israel gradually came to believe that there was only one God. Furthermore, unlike other peoples who chose which god they would follow, this God had *chosen them* to be his special people. Their understanding developed slowly over the centuries, with many false starts and setbacks, but they gradually came to a clearer knowledge of the nature of God: he was not interested in sacrifice and ritual for their own sake, was constantly surprising, and was just as likely to be present in 'sheer silence' as in a great storm (1 Kings 19:11–13). And while God was utterly 'other', beyond human understanding, at the same time he was passionately concerned in the fate of his chosen people. Jesus' subsequent teaching further deepened the mystery of this God, who is powerful beyond imagining, but at the same time was prepared to be vulnerable and to come into the created world in the form of a baby. Most important of all, Jesus revealed that God loves every single one of the creatures he has made.

I know from personal experience that it can take a long time, with many setbacks, to heal the inadequate or false images of God of our childhood. There seem to be stages in doing so. An anthropomorphic image of a loving God as a friend, or parent or lover is often the first stage on the healing journey. This is a helpful but limited image. As the relationship with God deepens, this image may fade and God seems to disappear, in a way that can test one's faith, and is sometimes referred to as 'the dark night of the soul'. My only explanation is that at this point God may be drawing us deeper into the mystery of whatever God *is*. Julian, the priest who married my wife and me in a small village in Botswana, later went to live deeper in the desert. His greatest desire was to bring the message of Jesus to the Basarwa people of the Kalahari (often, incorrectly, referred to as the 'Bushmen'), who are one of the most isolated and deprived groups of people in the world, essentially by living among them and learning their language.[3] When we visited him there, many years later, he told us that he got up early every morning and meditated for three hours. He commented: 'I am only just scratching the surface.' Thomas Aquinas (1225–1274), a priest-theologian, but also one of the world's greatest philosophers, said that God does not exist in any sense in which we understand the word 'existence'. In accepting the impossibility of fully comprehending what

God is, I do think that many thoughtful agnostics are more intellectually honest than those professing Christians whose faith has not deepened since their childhood.

God the Creator, God within us

All Christian doctrine consists of paradoxes enclosing mysteries. Even as we may contemplate the universe with its uncountable number of stars, some of them billions of light years away from us, we believe that God is beyond all of this, beyond anything we can possibly imagine in the created world.[4] Indeed, God is the author of this Creation. On the other side of the paradox God is closer to us than we are to ourselves, knows us better than we know ourselves and is infinitely in love with each one of us. I love the beautiful aphorism: 'What did God say when you were born?' 'Wow, why didn't I think of that before?' Other philosophical traditions have touched on the same mystery. It is, for example, expressed in the first verse of the ancient Chinese poem the *Tao Te Ching*:

The Tao that can be told

Is not the eternal Tao.

The name that can be named

Is not the eternal Name.[5]

This loving God is reaching out to everyone without exception, including those who profess no belief in God and those of us for whom the images we have held since childhood are no longer helpful or may even be harmful.

An aspect of exploring our image of God is to discern what it is that is life-giving for us, for God is the source of life, and God reveals his presence to all of us through whatever it is that personally animates us. This life-giving experience may be nothing 'religious' at all. It may be football, or art or gardening, or even mathematics. As my atheist piano teacher once said to me: 'My spirituality is in music.' Certainly music is a way in which people around the world touch some feeling, experience or awareness that is otherwise impossible to express in words. I believe that many people have this awareness from time to time of something intangible, beyond themselves, but they would certainly resist the notion that it is an experience of God. And during the COVID-19 pandemic in 2020–21 we became aware of the numbers of people, in hospitals and care homes particularly, for whom caring for other people was a deeply life-giving experience, and who acted out of unconditional love, even when that put them in danger themselves. Many of them would not accept any suggestion that they were responding to a God-given call, but would simply say: 'This is my job; this is what I do,' while also acknowledging the deep satisfaction that doing it gave them.

Passing on the Good News

So, does it really matter if we don't 'believe in' God? Ultimately, I think that what is more important than whether or not we believe in God is the complete trustworthiness of the fact that God believes in us. The author of the First Epistle of John – believed to have been the same person who wrote John's Gospel – said:

> God's love was revealed among us in this way: God sent his only Son into the world so that we might live through him. In this is love, not that we loved God but that he loved us and sent his Son to be the atoning sacrifice for our sins. Beloved, since God loved us so much, we also ought to love one another. No one has ever seen God; if we love one another, God lives in us and his love is perfected in us. (1 John 4:9–12)

If your image of God is that of a powerful, distant, even vengeful figure, then it is far better to reject such a belief. If, by contrast, your image of God is of a vulnerable, infinitely loving presence, closer to us than we are to ourselves – as I believe, despite all my questions and uncertainties – then, yes, I want everyone to share in that belief.

Sadly, the non-believer will not always find this vibrant image of God in the Christian Churches. Many Churches and church services seem to have ceased really to engage with the unfathomable mysteries of the story they proclaim, and have fallen back instead into a bland repetition of tired formulas and even a tendency to pick and choose which parts of Jesus' teaching to follow. So a challenge for the Churches now is to find new language and new channels for spreading the Good News, perplexing and demanding as it is, in ways that people can hear.[6] This does not mean that the Churches and their services do not offer church-goers spiritual sustenance – for God is not constrained by the limitations of forms of worship devised by human beings – but they do fail to attract and draw in new people – those who are puzzled by life and curious to make some sense of it. We shall explore these questions in greater depth later.

Nevertheless, any committed Christian, who is animated by the 'Good News' (the literal meaning of the word 'Gospel') of Jesus, cannot but long to pass this on to others – just as on Pentecost Day, after Jesus had departed from the world, the frightened apostles and disciples, who were hiding in an upper room, were touched by the Spirit, and immediately piled out of the room to preach to the diverse crowd outside (Acts 2:1–36). But *how* we pass on the Good News will depend on the time and circumstances. Francis of Assisi said: 'Preach always and sometimes use words.' Jesus' life and his teaching concern how we and others should live, individually and in community, how God is present with us, and how, finally, this will completely change the world – in short, how we can become *fully human*. His teaching was not primarily about moral codes or doctrinal beliefs or how to get to heaven, but rather about how to live a fulfilled life here and now. In our present society, this teaching may be more appropriately passed on through deeds than through words – a topic to which we shall return in the final Part of this book.

Jesus himself did not always seem to feel a need to preach. I am struck by how often in the Gospel stories Jesus encounters or heals someone who then disappears from the story. Apart from those he chooses to be his followers, he does not often say: 'Now stick around and I'll teach you more.' Perhaps a single healing encounter with the living Jesus is enough to change a whole life, and the people who experienced this did not need to be taught any more, or be told to go and tell others what had happened to them; they would just do that out of thankfulness. Indeed, in chapter 6 we shall explore the experience that many people still have of being touched by the divine, or at least something beyond normal experience, just briefly, but which they retain as a memory for the rest of their lives. Or perhaps, as in other places in the Gospel stories, Jesus is simply manifesting God's confidence in the people God has created – despite our tendency towards evil and sin. Imagine the powerful impact of Jesus as he stands on a hillside in front of a crowd of poor, powerless, disregarded men and women, and no doubt plenty of ragamuffins among them, and says: 'You are the light of the world' (Matthew 5:14). There is something to learn here of the 'slow work of God', which we shall encounter in the next chapter.

Although God's love does not discriminate, he does seem to choose people for particular tasks. And God sometimes picks out the most unexpected people: Moses with a speech impediment, who was chosen to lead the Israelites out of Egypt towards their promised land; Mary a poor young virgin, destined to be the mother of Jesus; John the Baptist, a wild man of the desert, who foreshadowed Jesus' own teaching; Simon (Peter) and Andrew, fishermen by the lakeside who became the first apostles; Matthew the tax collector, who abruptly left his counting table also to become an apostle; or Mary Magdalene, who was the first witness of the Resurrection.[7] Sometimes those who were chosen wanted to reject the call – Moses asked God to send someone else instead of him, but God persisted. Of course, we do not know about those who were chosen and *did* reject the call. God does not impose.

Some of the ancillary characters in the Gospels, those who are given a name, may also have been chosen, through a seemingly casual encounter with Jesus, to serve God's purpose, even though we cannot tell why it was they who were called on. They perhaps became Jesus' followers and were thus known to the later writers of the Gospels. Obvious candidates are Simon of Cyrene, who was pulled out of the crowd, no doubt because he was a foreigner, to help carry Jesus' cross; or Joseph of Arimathea, a rich man who buried Jesus after the Crucifixion. One could also mention the blind beggar Bartimaeus; the tax collector, Zacchaeus; or Nicodemus, who came at night-time to talk to Jesus.

The nature of God

I cannot leave these reflections on the mysterious nature of God, without touching on another mystery consistently preached by Christianity – the doctrine of the Trinity. There is only one God, but that God consists of three persons: Father, Son and Holy Spirit. This doctrine emerges from the early Christians' struggle to understand what Jesus meant when he talked of his Father, his Abba, and of the Spirit who would come after him. The exact formulation of the doctrine of the Trinity that eventually appeared was controversial and indeed contributed to the split between the Roman Church and the Orthodox Church in 1054.

There is a wonderful story about St Augustine (354–430), who spent thirty years writing a treatise about the Trinity, trying to conceive an intelligible explanation of the mystery.

He was walking by the seashore one day contemplating and

trying to understand the mystery of the Holy Trinity when he saw a small boy running back and forth from the water to a spot on the seashore. The boy was using a sea shell to carry the water from the ocean and place it into a small hole in the sand. Augustine approached him and asked, 'My boy, what are doing?' 'I am trying to bring all the sea into this hole,' the boy replied with a sweet smile. 'But that is impossible, my dear child, the hole cannot contain all that water,' said Augustine. The boy paused in his work, stood up, looked into the eyes of the Saint, and replied, 'It is no more impossible than what you are trying to do – comprehend the immensity of the mystery of the Holy Trinity with your small intelligence.'

A copy of the Rublev icon

Whereupon the boy disappeared.[8]

Artists have also struggled to depict the mystery of the Trinity – often falling back on a rather stylised image, with the Holy Spirit in the form of a dove hovering between an elderly Father and Jesus, his Son. More imaginative is the famous *Rublev* icon,[9] in which the three angels, who are generally considered to be an image of the Trinity and who are entertained by Abraham (Genesis 18:1–15), are shown seated around Abraham's table. It is said that the small rectangle near the bottom of the picture was originally a mirror in which observers saw themselves, so that they too were drawn into the scene and thus into intimacy with the Trinitarian God. At St Beuno's Spirituality Centre in north Wales, there is a wooden sculpture of the Trinity, represented as three dancing figures, separate but intertwined with one another. It is African and is, appropriately, carved from a single piece of wood.

Unfortunately, many Christians simply elide over this mystery, finding it perhaps too complicated, or maybe even unnecessary for their particular faith. Personally, I find it helpful to think of the Trinity not so much as three *persons* but as three *relationships*. Imagine two people deeply in love and committed to each other sitting, perhaps quietly, together. Nothing needs to be said between them. God, I believe, is present in this encounter, but where exactly? The answer is precisely in the relationship – the love that flows back and forth between them. For God is Love, and love cannot exist except in the context of relationship. Any image of a single-person God, as Islam has, is, for me, inadequate and cannot possibly express this truth. Relationship is at the core of whatever God is, so I'm a firm believer in the Trinity.

Yet, at a different level, the idea of a Trinitarian God is problematic. For, whatever image of God we hold, we believe that God 'exists' outside of Creation. But the mathematical concept of 'number' must be something that is created. The number 3 does not exist outside of Creation. So, to apply the created number 3 to an uncreated God cannot be correct. I suppose the only thing I can say is that this description of the Trinity is the best way that we, with our limited human comprehension, can express and understand the essentially incomprehensible God. Ultimately, the doctrine of the Trinity is simply a deep metaphor for some aspect of God that we do not fully understand. I make this point not because the nature of the Trinity needs to detain us – either in this text or in our exploration of the presence of God – but as a caution against too easily accepting a comfortable, even simplistic, explanation of an unfathomable truth.

1   I do not like the term 'spiritual director', but it is difficult to find another. 'Friend' is too weak; 'guide' implies that the person is

following a well-known path, whereas it should be God who shows the way; 'accompanier' is better, but is a rather clumsy neologism.

2   Hughes, op. cit., p. 34

3   This is well known as a 'click' language. Julian explained to us that there are many different clicks – thirty-two, if I remember well. He said that his Basarwa friends would fall about laughing when he tried to get them right.

4   I am told, in fact, that: 'There are roughly as many stars in our observable universe as there are molecules in a tablespoon of water' (David Broadhurst, private communication, 15 November 2020).

5   Lao tzu, *Tao Te Ching*; the edition quoted here is translated by Stephen Mitchell (New York: HarperCollins, 1999), p. 1.

6   For example, John Pungente and Monty Williams, in their book *Finding God in the Dark* (Boston: Pauline Books and Media, 2004) advocate the use of film as a way of engaging with Christian mysteries: 'Today, the media that shape us are film and television … Film proposes to us forms of the world and ethical ways of living in the world it creates. When we watch a film we are not just being entertained, we are being formed and shaped. We are exposing ourselves to narratives that shape what is possible, and we live out these possibilities' (p. 14).

7   Mary Magdalene is popularly believed to have been a converted sinner. In fact, there is no biblical evidence for this. She is more likely to have been a woman of independent means from the town of Magda. It is said that if the apostles had actually invented the story of the Resurrection, they would not have chosen a woman as a witness because, under Jewish law at the time, a woman's evidence carried only half the weight of that of a man.

8   As retold by Marian Horvat at https://www.traditioninaction.org/religious/h065rp.Shell.html

9   A painting by the Russian artist Andrei Rublev, dating from the first quarter of the fifteenth century, and now in the State Tretyakov Gallery in Moscow.

3 Creation, Evolution and Time

Creation and life

The very first verses of the Bible, at the beginning of the book of Genesis, tell a story of God creating the stars, the Earth, all the creatures of the Earth and finally humankind over a six-day period (Genesis 1:1–31). It is a story. Modern physics tells the story of the Big Bang, which happened about 13.7 billion years ago, when, seemingly from nothingness, matter appeared; this account continues with original matter, or rather energy, eventually becoming stars, planets and so on. From here, so far as the Earth is concerned, evolutionary biology takes over. Molecules coalesce into complex chemicals and basic living organisms, such as viruses and bacteria. Finally, living cells appear, then living creatures, and so on until the emergence of *Homo sapiens*, a mere two to three hundred thousand years ago.

We can choose whether or not we wish to equate the Big Bang with the moment of Creation, though we should notice that the one account concerns the 'how' of things, the other the 'why' of things. Still, there is a striking similarity between the two accounts, especially in that both comprise different stages. What we do know is that in physics it makes no sense to ask: 'What was there before the Big Bang?' just as in theology it makes no sense to ask: 'What was there before Creation?' This reminds me of the occasion when our then 4-year-old son asked his mother: 'Mummy, what would there be if space didn't exist?' She was driving him at the time and replied: 'You had better ask your father.'

My own take on this – whether theological or scientific – is that the possibility of 'life' is inherent in all matter. Theologically, matter and spirit, or 'soul', are inherent in all of Creation which yearns and strains, through evolution, towards the life-giving Creator. In scientific terms, everything seems to 'strive'

– for want of a better word – towards increasing complexity.[1] Elementary particles to atoms; atoms to molecules; molecules to cells and so on. This is evolution in action. And at each stage, whatever we mean by 'life' becomes increasingly manifest, with (so far) self-aware and transcendent-aware humanity as the most advanced stage in this progression. In discussing these ideas in *A Brief History of Everything*, Ken Wilber points out that as complexity emerges, the underlying elements do not lose their identity. So, atoms in a molecule remain atoms; molecules in a cell remain molecules; cells in the human body remain cells. And importantly, atoms in a molecule do not 'know' they form part of something else; they are still atoms. Likewise, the cells making up the human body do not 'know' they constitute part of a self-aware human being. But equally molecules depend on the prior existence of atoms, cells on molecules, the human body on cells and so on.[2]

In her delightful and highly readable book *Gaia's Dance: The Story of Earth and Us*, Elisabet Sahtouris points out that two processes actually seem to be at work in evolution.[3] The first is the well-known Darwinian idea of a *competitive* 'survival of the fittest'. But this cannot explain everything; for example, many evolutionary biologists think that such a complicated organ as the eye could not have evolved merely as a result of competitive evolution. So, the second process is an inherent *cooperative* tendency; at all stages of evolution the relevant entities seem to merge cooperatively into something more complex, more advanced – molecules into a cell, for example. Out of this process recognisable life slowly emerges.

This discussion invites the questions: has evolution stopped, and, if not, what will the next stage of evolutionary complexity be? Certainly, humanity has continued to evolve since the first arrival of *Homo sapiens*, with, in particular, an increasing ability for abstract, conceptual thought, an awareness of the feelings and motivations of others and perhaps psycho-social understanding. The German philosopher Karl Jaspers identified the period from about 800–300 BC as the 'Axial Age'. During this period, a surge of interest in the meaning of human existence and in abstract religious thought occurred, in an apparently unrelated manner, in several different parts of the world – China, India, Persia, Greece and among the Hebrew people of the Old Testament. Was this evolutionary development a necessary preparation for God's choice to become present in his Creation a few hundred years later? Human society has undoubtedly become increasingly complex over time, evolving from the small clan groups that characterised early human society to the sense we all now have of being part of a worldwide human community. This is not a smooth process; at the time of writing, social and political cooperation across humanity seem in many ways to be going backwards.

And what will the next phase of evolution be like? No doubt we shall retain our identity as individual human beings, much as we are at present; we are not expected to grow another pair of arms, however useful this might be to young mothers. Rather, the next stage will probably concern the further evolution of human society as a whole. But, given that we are self-aware, will we be able to observe this evolution happening, see our individual selves increasingly as part of a whole, in a way that the cells in our bodies are unable to do? Will we be able to understand what humanity has become or is becoming? And – perhaps the most important question of all, which is also deeply theological – will we, collectively have any control over this stage of evolution, or will we just passively have to accept it? In Part IV of this book, I discuss the common problems faced by the whole of humanity. Will we evolve sufficiently to overcome them collectively, which at the moment we are signally failing to do?

One of the first thinkers to discuss these ideas was the French Jesuit priest and eminent paleontologist Pierre Teilhard de Chardin. His thinking straddled science and theology. He saw humankind evolving towards what he called the 'Omega Point', which, according to my understanding, he identified as the ultimate destiny of humanity and indeed of the whole of Creation – the final completion of Jesus' Kingdom. His Jesuit superiors forbad him to publish these ideas during his lifetime, but he passed his papers on to a relative, who published his work after his death in 1955. When his book *The Phenomenon of Man* did appear,[4] it created a minor sensation. I remember as a young boy hearing my father and grandfather discussing it. My grandfather, who was a staunch Catholic, said he had read it thoroughly and had carefully marked in the margins all the many heresies. Now I, together with many other Christians, am quite comfortable with these theological ideas, even though I do not understand them fully. Indeed, we might say that the idea of the whole of Creation striving and evolving towards the life of the Creator was adumbrated two millennia ago by Paul, who in his Letter to the Romans, talks of all of Creation 'groaning in labour pains until now' (Romans 8:22).

Our time, God's time

The foregoing discussion may seem to have taken us rather a long way from the theology of God's Creation. Let me move on to another problem, deriving from modern physics. A big unresolved question in physics is how to reconcile and unify Einstein's theory of relativity, which tries to explain space and time at the very large scale, with quantum theory, which attempts the same at the smallest possible scale.

Relativity may be complicated to understand but is essentially deterministic: precise equations can be written that tell you exactly what will happen. Moreover, space, or distance, is continuous; it can be divided into ever smaller units *ad infinitum*. In contrast, quantum theory is essentially probabilistic: how a small particle will behave is determined by probability. Yet when a very large number of very small particles are acting together – as is the case with everything that we can actually observe, even down to the smallest of objects or living things – the combined outcome of their individual probabilities can be predicted with a very high degree of certainty. Thus we are completely unaware of these probabilistic events in ordinary life. Moreover, physical 'things' ultimately consist of discrete particles that cannot be further subdivided.[5]

One of the respected theoretical physicists attempting the unification of these two very different theories is the Italian Carlo Rovelli. He is a gifted communicator, and something of a philosopher, and has written several books explaining the problem in layman's terms.[6] The models he works on suggest that, as with the very small particles of quantum theory, *distance* may also consist of very small units rather than being infinitely divisible as relativity assumes.

Rovelli says that, according to this hypothesis, as he and his colleagues work through their calculations, the variable called 'time' simply disappears; it is no longer a necessary concept. What is essential to know is that constant *change* is a fundamental concept of physical reality, but these changes are not governed or measured by something called 'time'. Indeed, even according to relativity theory, 'time' had already become a rather slippery idea. Many of us are familiar with the notion, derived from relativity, that if someone travels at great speed to a distant star and then returns to earth, the amount of 'time' that has passed for them will be different from the 'time' that has passed for those who remained on Earth. In short, 'time' may be real to our experience but is not necessary for a deep understanding of the physical world. It is not a fundamental parameter of Creation. Rather 'time' emerges as some sort of 'illusion' because of our inability to comprehend what is taking place at the level of individual particles.[7]

We should not let these ideas bother us in daily life; we do not yet have the vocabulary to express them in ordinary language and I shall continue to refer to 'time' in the usual way in the rest of this book. But we should hold them in the back of our minds – just as we should hold the doctrine of the Trinity as a metaphor for something beyond our understanding, as I argued in the previous chapter. After all, we say that the sun rises in the morning, passes across the sky from east to west and sets in the evening. What we all now know, as a result of earlier scientific work, is that the sun does not move at all; it is the rotation of the earth that causes this phenomenon. Similarly, as we contemplate various theological mysteries that 'do not make any sense', we should have the humility to realise that much of what we experience in daily life does not make any sense either. To borrow the title of another of Rovelli's books: *Reality Is Not What It Seems*.[8]

I have now reached the limit of my own understanding of these theories. But they did come as a revelation to me. One of the difficulties of comprehending our Christian faith is the meaning of 'eternity'. We generally believe that after death we will live 'in eternity', and that God exists as an eternal being. We struggle to imagine this as time just going on for ever and ever. Doesn't it get boring, the sameness of it all? But if time does not really exist then eternity must be something quite different, something we do not understand. Moreover, God exists in the eternal present. The whole story of Creation, the Fall, Redemption and the end of the world may appear to us to be separate events, but they are not marked out or limited by time.

One of the few sermons I can actually remember, was given by my sometime Jesuit schoolmaster Michael Ivens a few months before he died of a brain tumour, and after it had already made him blind. What it was about his delivery that impressed me I do not now recall. But his essential message was that God can work in infinitesimal fractions of time, even, for example, at the point of death. We know that the Good Thief on the cross next to Jesus is the only biblical character who was specifically promised eternal life at the moment of his death (Luke 23:39–43); we do not know the fate of the 'bad' thief on the other side of Jesus, or indeed of anyone else.

I used these various ideas when I was asked to give the oration at the funeral of my granddaughter Isobel Mari on 22 November 2012. She had lived for just three days. I said:

How do we make sense of all this; this birth and then tragic death three days later of Isobel Mari?

In the little bit of spiritual direction work that I do, by far the most important thing is to encourage people to have a sense of God's infinite love for each one of them – individually and uniquely – a sense in their guts rather than just in their head. Usually it does not come readily; it is a gift. But with that everything else falls into place. So in God's eyes, Isobel Mari was born a perfect creation. And God was, or I should say is, utterly in love with her, just as he, or she, is in love with each one of us gathered here. Every life is just as precious to him as every other.

So why did he not let her live?

The first thing to say is that God's sense or experience of time is completely different from ours. He can accomplish his purpose in a fraction of a second – what to us might seem to require a lifetime. So the life of Isobel Mari, just three days during which she did not even open her eyes to see the beautiful world into which she had been born, was just as worthwhile, just as fulfilled, as that of someone who dies at the ripe old age of a hundred. Of course, *we* cannot see it that way, indeed we may find the whole idea offensive – repellant even. We think: 'What a waste, a life unfulfilled.' But as the prophet Isaiah reminds us: 'my thoughts are not your thoughts, nor are your ways my ways, says the Lord'

(Isaiah 55:8–9). And Isobel will certainly be remembered long into the future, just as our family still remembers and talks about her great-great-aunt Maureen who also died young nearly a hundred years ago.

And just consider what she did accomplish in her brief life – all that love and thoughtfulness and care and coming together, the deepening of the bonds of love between us, that she brought forth from us all. All this will last and will sustain us and carry us forward into the future. Admittedly this was done unintentionally, unconsciously – but then reflect for a moment how much of the good we ourselves may do from time to time is done unintentionally. Sometimes it is sufficient just to be who we are and little Isobel was just being who she was.

It also works the other way. God sometimes seems incredibly slow to act, as suggested by a well-known prayer of Teilhard de Chardin in which he says that we have to 'trust in the slow work of God'.

The Bible is full of stories of men who lived to a great age, or of women giving birth long after their usual child-bearing years were over. Methuselah was said to have been 969 years old when he died (Genesis 5:27), Sarah, Abraham's wife, was a great age when her son Isaac was born (Genesis 21:2), and Abraham himself died at the age of 175. We are not meant to take these statements literally. They are stories attempting to convey truths. One truth might be that these were highly respected figures, old age being a reason for respect. Another, more important, truth is that God works in God's own time, which can seem impossible in human terms. On this, the Jesuit writer James Martin has an amusing little parable about God being like a carpenter in a small village:

If you ask the townspeople where to turn for carpentry

work or repairs, they will say: 'There is only one person to call. He does excellent work. He's careful, he's precise, he's conscientious, he's creative, he makes sure everything fits and he tailors his work exactly to fit your needs. There's just one problem: he takes *forever*.'[9]

The Dominican priest Timothy Radcliffe summarises the question in a different way in a passage that will again seem relevant in the last part of this book, when we discuss Christian action in the world:

Why does the Lord delay? Why do the poor still have to go on crying out for justice two thousand years after the coming of Christ? Why does not God bring about a world in which all of humanity may flourish now?...

We do not know the answer to that but at the very least we must live with the urgency of the question. Any answer that looks like an explanation of vast suffering is likely to appear horrible, even blasphemous, as if so much human misery could be part of some monstrous divine plan. All that we can do ... is share in that clamouring of the poor for a better world and do all that we can to hasten its coming.

Perhaps one tiny element of a response is in deepening our understanding of how God comes. One reason why God takes so much time is because he is not a god. Our God is not a powerful, celestial superman.... The coming of God is not like the cavalry galloping to our rescue. God comes from within, in our deepest interiority. He is, as St Augustine said, closer to us than we are to ourselves.[10]

1 Developing this idea further could inform the controversial question that lies behind current debates on abortion: at what point does human life begin?

2 Ken Wilber, *A Brief History of Everything* (Boston: Shambala

Publications, Inc., 1996), p. 32

3   Elisabet Sahtouris, *Gaia's Dance: the story of earth and us* (n.p., n. pub., 2015)

4   Pierre Teilhard de Chardin, *Le phénomène humain* (Paris: Éditions du Seuil, 1955); translated by Bernard Wall as *The Phenomenon of Man* (London: Wm. Collins Sons & Co., 1959).

5   I am ignoring here that these particles do not always behave like 'particles' at all but rather as waves.

6   The one I have read (in translation) is Carlo Rovelli, *L'ordine del tempo* (Milan: Adelphi, 2014); translated by Erica Segre and Simon Carnell, as *The Order of Time* (London: Allen Lane, 2019).

7   The concept of 'temperature' is perhaps similar. It is something that we feel and can measure, but merely results from the combined energetic motion of billions of individual particles. It has no objective reality beyond that.

8   Carlo Rovelli, *La realtà non è come ci appare: la struttura elementare delle cose* (Milan: Raffaello Cortina Editore, 2014); translated by Simon Carnell and Erica Segre, as *Reality Is Not What It Seems: the journey to quantum gravity* (London: Allen Lane, 2016)

9   James Martin SJ, *The Jesuit Guide to (Almost) Everything: a spirituality for real life* (New York: HarperCollins, 2012), p. 99

10 Timothy Radcliffe (ed.), *Just One Year: prayer and worship through the Christian year* (London: Darton Longman & Todd, 2006), p. 24

.

Part II: Having a Relationship with God

Prayer is like watching for the
Kingfisher. All you can do is
Be where he is likely to appear, and
Wait.
Often, nothing much happens;
There is space, silence and
Expectancy.
No visible sign, only the
Knowledge that he's been there,
And may come again.
Seeing or not seeing cease to matter,
You have been prepared.
But sometimes, when you've almost
Stopped expecting it,
A flash of brightness
Gives encouragement.[1]

We have looked at the mystery of who or what God is and how Jesus, throughout his life, death and Resurrection, and through his radical teaching, turned the wisdom of the world on its head and showed us the way to God. We have glimpsed the often-unfathomable ways in which God makes his presence felt in the world he Created and in relation to humankind. Now we are going to explore how human beings react to God, and different ways of opening ourselves to relationship with him.

1   Lewin, op. cit., p. 31

4 Prayer as Relationship

The desire for God

Prayer, in one form of another, is a feature of all the great religions. Even Buddhism which doesn't believe in God in the usual sense of that word, places huge emphasis on meditation. Yet we, at least in Western culture, don't talk much about prayer or about our personal experience of praying. It's a taboo subject in our secular age. Nevertheless, I personally think that most people, even those who profess no belief in a God, are drawn to pray – or to be in contact with the unknown Other – more often than they admit, and – like me – usually pray to ask for help.

When I started to make the Spiritual Exercises of St Ignatius, my wise spiritual director gave me a copy of a little book, *God and You: Prayer as a Personal Relationship*, by the American Jesuit, William A. Barry. It was an eye-opener to me and I've returned to it often ever since. I frequently recommend it to other people who want to learn about prayer. Early in the book, Barry recounts an anecdote that recalls our earlier discussion of our image of God:

> When my mother was dying of cancer, she said that she prayed every night that God would take her in her sleep. I asked her what God was like, and she answered, 'He's a lot better than he's made out to be.' She was referring, of course, to many of the things said about God from pulpits and in talks. Her own experience had taught her differently about God ... simply from praying a lot.... She said something like this: 'Sometimes while you're saying your prayers, you go deep and you know he's listening to you and you to him.' Apparently my mother had got to know the living God and found him a good deal more benign than he had been made out to be.[1]

The whole of Barry's book is about building a relationship with the benign living God. Guided by it, I have evolved my own way of thinking about getting to know God.

As there are many ways of building a relationship, so there are many ways of praying and we will choose different ways on different occasions. The most important thing is to have the desire to pray – to deepen the relationship with God. A relationship involves two people, and the other person in this particular relationship hugely desires to enter into our friendship and invites us to let him do so, just as, at the Last Supper, Jesus calls his disciples his friends: 'I have called you friends because I have made known to you everything that I have heard from my Father' (John 15:15). God may indeed instil or encourage this desire in us, but he does not impose on us or oblige us. The medieval anchorite and mystic Julian of Norwich talks of God's immense 'courtesy'.[2] In the story of the road to Emmaus, when Jesus' disciples and their new companion (who was in fact the risen Jesus, though they did not at first recognise him) reach their destination, he makes as if to go on – not presuming on their hospitality – until they invite him to stay with them:

> As they came near to the village to which they were going, he walked ahead as if he were going on. But they urged him strongly, saying, 'Stay with us, because it is almost evening and the day is now nearly over.' (Luke 24:29)

All that's required on our part is to have the desire to deepen the relationship, which actually means giving it time and attention, normally through what we have come to call prayer. Then we can largely leave the shaping of it in the care of the other person – in this case God, who has much more experience of how to build such a friendship than we have. In this sense – again as my spiritual director told me (much to my astonishment at the time) – when we pray, it is actually God who prays in us.

There are several implications of this. First, having the desire to pray is the most important requirement; the actual technique or form of prayer that we use – the way we express that desire – is relatively unimportant. It can range from solitary, silent, emptying meditation, through spontaneous talking to God or the recitation of a formal prayer, such as the 'Our Father', all the way to communal singing of hymns together in church or elsewhere. We may be drawn to different forms of prayer at different moments, and what may feel appropriate at one time may not be at another. The repetition of a simple formula, known as a mantra,[3] may help us to empty our minds and open us up to God; similarly, occupying our hands in a routine activity may also be a useful aid.[4] Second, prayer may be more or less *intense*, again depending on the circumstances. Certainly, there are occasions when we desperately cry out to God to help someone in need or to sustain us in a particular difficulty. At the other extreme, any normal activity can be turned into a form of prayer; we can ask God simply to be with us as we wash the dishes: perhaps being thankful for the food we have eaten or reflecting on the service we may have offered to others in preparing it.[5] In the next chapter we shall discuss pilgrimage. The whole venture of going on a pilgrimage might be considered a form of prayer, but most of the time it is hardly intense. Third, praying should not be a source of anxiety, or at least no more so than the anxiety we may feel about any developing human relationship. Similarly, people sometimes say that prayer is *difficult*. I'm not sure about that; there should not be any difficulty in a relationship with an utterly benign Other. But I fear some guides and books on prayer, with instructions on how to do it 'correctly', may actually reinforce this sense of difficulty. Finally, prayer is not about *achieving* anything. Our society is so strongly characterised by goals and achievements wherever we look – except perhaps in our personal relationships. How unusual it would be to set goals or targets in a genuine human relationship of love and trust! So it is with prayer.

How to pray

Consequently, a good way to learn how to pray is to think about how the best human relationships work and are deepened, and apply the same approach to prayer. We are, after all, made in the image of God, as the very first verses of the Bible tell us: 'God created humankind in his image. In the image of God he created them' (Genesis 1:27). So we can learn something about the, ultimately unfathomable, God, and about prayer, by looking at our human nature. For example, something that makes people anxious over prayer is 'distractions'. But we all get distractions in life: it is part of being a thinking, feeling person, and God knows this. What is important is not to be waylaid by the distracting thoughts. Let's take the analogy of visiting a sick friend in hospital. We may say something like: 'Well, I wanted to come and see you and I've got half an hour before I need to go.' In that half-hour we try to focus on the other person. Our phone may ring: a distraction. We may answer briefly, but if we then start to ignore the person we're visiting and enter into a long conversation with the person on the phone, then we are no longer deepening the relationship with our sick friend. The same is true in prayer. Accept that distractions may come, but gently push them away for the moment. At the same time, we need to be aware that these distracting thoughts may actually be God's response to our prayer. It would be a shame to miss that! But the best thing may be just to make a mental note of the possibility and come back to it later when our prayer time is over. In the Ignatian spiritual tradition this is referred to as the 'review after prayer'.

My analogy of visiting a sick friend is also an illustration of giving time and space to the other person in a human relationship and arranging for this to be possible. The arrangement might involve just sitting silently together, talking, or doing some activity together. We can apply the same approach to prayer. For private prayer at home you might dedicate a particular place in your house to prayer, or you might have an object that can be taken with you wherever you go to pray – something as simple as an icon (a sacred picture) or a candle that you light for the duration of your prayer time, as an indication that during this time this is what you are about. In communal prayer, rituals and routines may help us to enter into prayer, religious liturgy being the most obvious example. And having decided how much time we have to pray – whether two minutes or an hour – we should stick to that decision, even if 'nothing is happening'. When we visit our sick friend, we might reasonably start by saying: 'I'm in a bit of a rush; I've just got half an hour.' But we don't say after a short while: 'This is boring. I'm going.' It's the same with prayer.

There is also no reason why we shouldn't turn other activities, such as going for a walk or doing a painting, into prayer. But we do need to be deliberate about doing so, dedicating the activity as a time of prayer, inviting God to join with us and noticing what thoughts or feelings might come to us as we engage in the activity. Although I have not often prayed through painting, when I have, I've found that the prayer seems to go deeper within me than at most other times, as I reflect on what God is saying to me: why did I choose this colour here? Why did I make that line or shape there? And so on. Many years later, I can recall the experiences and what they seemed to mean. At the end of the thirty-day retreat that I mentioned earlier, one of the other participants, who throughout the retreat had prayed almost entirely through painting, mounted an exhibition, about sixty paintings all told – two a day. They were abstract and largely meaningless to the rest of us, but the woman concerned could talk of her emotions and feelings associated with each one as she reviewed it.

As well as variety, we need patience. Relationships take time to develop. They have their ups and downs. They need to be deepened in different ways at different times. God does not wish to overwhelm us, but rather to come gently and slowly into our lives. Imagine encountering someone in life who announced suddenly that they were going to love you unconditionally and deeply. I think most of us would initially back off: 'Hang on! I'm not ready for that.' Of course, such deep love does occur in human relationships but, as with our relationship with God, it emerges slowly, often over half a lifetime.

I would summarise this discussion in two general rules. First if you're not sure about some aspect of prayer or what to expect, then think about what works in the best human relationships. And, second, pray as you can, not as you can't.

For many people, perhaps Catholics especially, God is so remote, so 'other', that the only way they feel they can pray is through intermediaries – usually through Mary, or some favourite saint. And there is no doubt that God reaches out to those people through the intermediary, who may not even need to be someone formally recognised as a 'saint'. I once met a woman who faced multiple problems. She felt great consolation in praying to her deceased grandmother, who, she said, was the only person who had ever really loved her.

Petitionary prayer

In starting this chapter, I speculated that prayer for most people is usually asking God for something. Of course, the Church has other forms of prayer, through its religious services, expressing perhaps worship, praise or thanksgiving. But I do wonder, when we sing: 'Praise him, praise him', how often that sentiment is really coming from the heart, and how often it's just a repetition of the words – I speak for myself here. And 'worship' is one of those words, like 'salvation', that the Church uses but which have lost much meaning in ordinary parlance. How many people could articulate what 'salvation' means to them in their day-to-day life? Perhaps it's right that some words are reserved largely for speaking about a transcendent being, who is ultimately beyond our understanding. But that kind of language may also be a way of keeping God at a distance, a way of suggesting that we cannot approach this God, who is completely 'other', with our usual words. And yet, when I read the Gospels, I find Jesus teaching in ordinary language, occasionally using rather earthy words (the impact of which may be lost in translation), and telling stories that reflect the dilemmas and lessons of human life. And Jesus repeatedly tells us, through parables, that it is perfectly okay to ask the Father for what we want through prayer. It is often said that a drowning man's prayer is not one of praise or thanksgiving but one of urgent petition.

Yet petitionary prayer is problematic. Asking God for some favour doesn't make God change his mind. A God who infinitely loves each one of us always desires what is best for us. God's loving action towards us is never a reward for good behaviour, and God does not cause bad things to happen to us as a punishment for our sinfulness. God never offers us second best, so our asking for something does not convince God to choose something better than he would otherwise have given us. Besides, if God exists outside time, as we discussed earlier, then the notion of *change* applied to God is meaningless.

Notwithstanding these difficulties, the idea of asking God for something – petitionary prayer – is deeply embedded in Christian understanding and theology, and, since we have Jesus' own injunction that we should ask the Father for what we need or want, there must be some meaning and purpose to it. Perhaps it is really a metaphor for something mysterious beyond our understanding. One possibility is that, rather than changing God, prayer changes us, or sometimes opens up new possibilities for God to act. None of us can be forced by someone who loves us to change our attitudes or behaviour. Yet we know from ordinary experience that often people in difficulty can only be helped once they have accepted their need. Perhaps it is sometimes the same with prayer; only when we accept our need can God's love do its work.

Moreover, sometimes prayer seems to be answered in ways

that are quite unexpected. A good friend of mine, who had become a practising Christian after slowly and carefully reading *God of Surprises*, was dying of stomach cancer. One day he was lying on his bed, in great pain, next to a downstairs open French window. A cat walked in through the window and sat on his stomach for a while. He found his pain soothed. He told me he had never seen that particular cat before and never saw it again. One need not attach any importance to such an incident, but he obviously did; otherwise he would not have told me about it. Was the cat an answer to his prayer – some sort of messenger from God? Who knows?

Prayer may also open channels of communication and support between human beings in ways we don't understand. Part of the difficulty here is that we live in a 'scientific', supposedly rational world, which tends to discount anything that cannot be subject to observation and measurement. We know, for example, about beauty and happiness and love, but they cannot be subject to scientific analysis. They cannot be measured or weighed or calculated. Perhaps there is also 'unscientific' communication between people, the very description of which as 'paranormal' demonstrates our scepticism about such phenomena. It seems likely that Indians in the Amazon jungle or the Aborigines of Australia would understand this better than we Westerners, who live with such an empirical mindset. As Pope Francis frequently emphasises, we need to learn much more from the marginalised people and cultures in this world.

In this sense – that prayer puts us in touch with one another's love and support – I believe that everyone prays. When, with no thought of, or belief in, God, we say or write to someone in trouble that we are 'thinking about them', what do we mean and intend, and what practical effect does it have? But the other person concerned finds it consoling or helpful. Why should that be? In our deterministic, scientific mindset, thinking of the other person can make absolutely no difference to their problem. So why do it or say it? But we instinctively do, and perhaps it opens up possibilities between people that are beyond our scientific understanding, and allows the loving God, whose existence the two parties involved may not even acknowledge, to be drawn into the situation.

Finally, God frequently 'answers' prayer not by 'fixing' things, but rather by changing our perceptions. John McMurray, the Scottish philosopher, has written:

> The maxim of illusory religion runs: Fear not, trust God and he will see that none of the things you are afraid of will happen to you. That of true religion runs: Fear not, the things you are afraid of might well happen to you, but they are nothing to be afraid of.[6]

The foregoing discussion may give the impression of prayer as a rather dry and unrewarding experience. It often is. But there can also be times of great joy and consolation, usually fleeting moments that nevertheless stay fixed in memory – a kiss of the Divine. I remember one particular occasion during a retreat when, as I was sitting supposedly praying, I simply fell asleep – which of course is perfectly okay. But as I woke up, I experienced a brief sensation of God just looking at me with great tenderness and love. I have never forgotten that. The young Dutch Jewish writer Etty Hillesum sometimes experienced joy in her prayer to a degree that is difficult for us to imagine. In the Westerbork internment camp on 18 August 1943, a few weeks before she was taken to Auschwitz and murdered, she wrote in her diary:

Etty Hillesum

> You have made me so rich, O God, please let me share out your beauty with open hands. My life has become an uninterrupted

dialogue with You, O God, one great dialogue. Sometimes when I stand in some corner of the camp, my feet planted on Your earth, my eyes raised towards Your heaven, tears sometimes run down my face, tears of deep emotion and gratitude. At night, too, when I lie in my bed and rest in You, O God, tears of gratitude run down my face, and that is my prayer.[7]

1   William A. Barry, *God and You: prayer as a personal relationship* (Mahwah, NJ: Paulist Press, 1987), p. 16

2   See Julian of Norwich, *Revelations of Divine Love*, edited by A. C. Spearing and Elizabeth Spearing (London: Penguin Classics, 1998).

3   A mantra that is frequently recommended is *maranatha*, which means 'Come, Lord Jesus' in Aramaic, the language that Jesus spoke.

4   Many Catholics pray the rosary, which seems to me to be an excellent form of prayer, though I don't often use it myself. The repetition of a prayer formula – in this case the 'Hail Mary' – helps to keep our mind away from other distractions. And the fingering of the rosary beads is a mechanical routine with the same purpose – as we count off five decades (sets of ten) repetitions of the prayer. This is then repeated three times as we reflect on the Joyful, Sorrowful and Glorious mysteries of Jesus' life. In this way the rosary also marks out a definite and limited prayer period.

5   In my Jesuit-run school, we were required to write AMDG (*Ad majorem Dei gloriam*, 'For the greater glory of God') at the top of every piece of work we did, and then LDS (*Laus Dei semper*, 'Praise be to God always') at the end. We did not think about it much at the time, but this was in principle a turning of the work into a form of prayer.

6   John Macmurray, *Persons in Relation* (London: Faber & Faber, 1961), p. 171

7   *Letters and Diaries of Etty Hillesum*, edited by Eva Hoffman, translated by Arnold J. Pomerans (London: Persephone, 1999), p. 395

5 Pilgrimage and the *Camino de Santiago*

Formal prayer, as we've been discussing, is all very well for those who are fortunate to have some sense of, some belief in, a personal, loving God. But for various reasons, including the current failures of our institutional Christian Churches, many people have lost or never found this sense. So for those looking elsewhere for God – though generally they would not use such an expression – there are other, more subtle and perhaps more appropriate possibilities. Pilgrimage is an example, which makes no demand for formal belief and is equally open to those who may or may not consider themselves to be believing Christians. Like prayer, pilgrimage is a feature of many of the great world religions, and Christianity is no exception. And even though, unlike prayer, only a small fraction of the 'faithful' have the opportunity to make a pilgrimage, I will argue that the *Camino de Santiago*, in particular, has features that should influence the Christian Church as it faces the future.

The *Camino de Santiago*

Many of those who embark on a pilgrimage would say that they are looking 'to find themselves', or to get in touch with a deeper meaning to their existence by turning away for a time from 'normal' life and following a more or less difficult undertaking. The word 'God' is not necessarily in their vocabulary. Yet, if we exclude those who sail solo around the world, cross the Antarctic, scale an impossible rock face, or undertake some similar challenge, pilgrims almost invariably choose to travel a path with some religious connection – whether it be the ancient walk to Canterbury that Chaucer recounted in his *Canterbury Tales*, or the new Australian pilgrimage route honouring Australia's own saint Mary McKillop.

My own experience is that of walking the *Camino de Santiago* (the Way of St James), for which there are many traditional departure points right across Europe, as far north as the Baltic Sea, all leading to Santiago in the Galician province of northern Spain. Most pilgrims, now start in St Jean-Pied-du-Port just on the French side of the Pyrenees, about 800 km (500 miles) from Santiago. When I walked the *Camino*, I started a further 800 km back, in France at Le Puy-en-Velay. I undertook my pilgrimage in stages over a period of six years – as many pilgrims do – and did not eschew all creature comforts – as do those who sleep out in the open or in church porches – usually staying overnight with my companions in small hotels or hostels.

Santiago is claimed to be the final resting place of St James the Apostle, brother of John, the purported author of John's Gospel. This claim is surrounded by a great deal of myth and legend and has no real historical justification. No matter. It seems likely that this pilgrimage route emerged around the eleventh century, when the Holy Land, a traditional pilgrimage destination in what is now Israel, was occupied by people practising Islam and was therefore closed off to Christians.

The classic pilgrimage route through Spain, the *Camino Francés* (the French Way) as it is known, is full of variety. The first day's walk – some 29 kilometres across the Pyrenees – can seem very daunting, not least if there is snow on the ground or mist in the air. But then you arrive with relief at the monastery of Roncesvalles and probably spend the night in the huge 500-bed hostel which the monks provide. You set off again early the next morning, perhaps after attending Mass in the monastery church and receiving the traditional *Camino* blessing. Over the next few days, the footpath takes you through rolling countryside, then to the centre of the city of Burgos with its magnificent but over-elaborate cathedral. After that, the long, flat, featureless *Meseta*, with just a few villages to pass through, takes several days. Perhaps this is the section where the lone pilgrim can most experience the graces and trials of solitude. This stage takes you to León, which also has a cathedral, Gothic in style and featuring nearly two thousand square metres of stained glass. Then as you enter the western province of Galicia the mountains reappear. You reach the highest point on the *Camino*, at 1530 metres, on Mount Irago (which is higher than the Pyrenees crossing you did some three weeks earlier). Near the summit stands an iron cross, the *Cruz de Ferro*. Here, as a symbol of the laying down of your burdens, you add the small stone you have been carrying all the way from wherever you started to the huge mound of stones at the foot of the cross. Finally, the *Camino* winds up and down through the farmland and small towns and villages of Galicia, becoming (sadly) somewhat commercialised as you get closer to Santiago. Finally, Santiago is in sight. The Way takes you around the end of the airport – from where most modern pilgrims make their return journey! At last you reach your destination, the huge plaza in front of the cathedral, where as often as not you meet by chance or arrangement some of the other pilgrims you've encountered along the Way. Many people then walk for a further four days to the coast at Muxia near Finisterre – the *Fin de la Tierra* (the end of the earth) – where in times past pilgrims would burn their dirty, louse-infected clothes and worn-out footwear on the clifftop.

For most pilgrims walking the Way is like a form of prayer; you take time out from normal life in order to be open to something new, something challenging and different – to be in touch somehow with the 'Other'. It is a spiritual experience, though more like a slow-burning fuse than a flash of enlightenment. For myself, I did not feel at the time that my pilgrimage was particularly spiritually rewarding. Indeed, my clearest memory of finally arriving at the cathedral in Santiago was not one of great joy or elation – which my companions were experiencing – but rather of a desperate need to find a toilet! Such is the stuff of real life. As with other forms of prayer, the fruits can come quietly and slowly much later. In my case, it happened like this. On the *Camino* in France, just outside the small village of Fonteilles, I had been inspired by a roadside memorial to a local man called Pepe Catusse, which consisted of a photograph of him and a short inscription, translated as follows:

> Friends, Pilgrims, Walkers over many years one of my greatest pleasures was to come to the *chemin* [the pilgrim path] to meet you, say hello, offer encouragement, chat for a minute, recount some stories ... I came very often to sit here but, since 5 April 2008 I have gone to join the thousands of stars marking out your route, and from on high, I am accompanying you.

On my return home I commented to my wife that sitting by the road talking to passing pilgrims must be a good way to die, to which her response was: 'In that case you'd better get on with it!'

Emmaüs at Arthez-de-Béarn

So, in 2014 we bought a house directly on the *Camino* in Arthez-de-Béarn in south-west France and in the front garden pitched the old family tent as a place of welcome for passing pilgrims. We reasoned that there was no lack of *gîtes* and *albergues* along the *Camino* for pilgrims to spend the night, and plenty of places for them to eat an evening meal, but there were only limited opportunities just for rest and conversation – spiritual or otherwise – along the Way. Two years later the old tent blew down in a storm. The following year, 2017, we replaced it with a small wooden shelter, complete with a coffee corner and a small 'oratory' or place of prayer.

The pilgrim shelter at Arthez-de-Béarn

Here pilgrims can pause for a while during the day – rest, talk with other pilgrims or the host, perhaps just reflect and pray, but also drink a coffee or eat their lunch. The centrepiece of our simple oratory is a copy of Caravaggio's painting, in the National Gallery in London, of the supper at Emmaus – a story to which I already referred in the previous chapter. The two disciples, deeply depressed and traumatised after the death of Jesus, on whom they had placed all their hopes, are walking – perhaps returning – to the village of Emmaus, several hours' walk from Jerusalem, when they meet up with a third person, who explains to them the mystery of Jesus' death and how it was foretold in the Jewish scriptures. Inspired by this conversation, on reaching their destination, they invite the stranger to stay with them. At supper he breaks bread whereupon they recognise him as the risen Jesus who at once disappears from their sight. They immediately get up and walk back up to Jerusalem in the dark to tell their story to the other disciples (Luke 24:13–35). It is one of my favourite Gospel stories and seems particularly appropriate for a pilgrim halt – the two disciples were on a journey when they met up with someone who changed their lives, just as, today, pilgrims often find renewal and enlightenment through meeting other pilgrims along the Way. Rather wonderfully, in this painting Caravaggio imagined one of the two disciples to be St James, as indicated by the scallop shell, the traditional symbol of a *Camino* pilgrim, that he is wearing.

Supported by a group of volunteers, who stay in the house when my wife and I are not there, we now welcome each year up to four hundred pilgrims. Some stay just a few minutes and perhaps take a coffee or use the toilet. Others stay longer and occasionally pray in the oratory. A few join us for morning prayer, which we hold at 8.30 each morning. All have their own individual stories. Most pilgrims are French but some have set off from their homes across Europe – Germany, Austria, Switzerland, even as far away as Poland – and have already been walking for many weeks.

Most of our visitors leave with a postcard of the Caravaggio painting or a small olive-wood 'holding cross' – that universal symbol of Christianity – which fits comfortably in the hand as they walk along. Some leave a coin or two in our jar, though we make no charge for anything. Almost all let us take their photo, which we put on the wall of the shelter, then they excitedly search for the photos of other pilgrims they've met on the Way. Some also give us permission to share their photo and story on the blog of our website.[1] A few send us emails or postcards when they reach Santiago and complete their pilgrimage. All display on their rucksacks the precious scallop shell, the traditional symbol of their sense of belonging to this particular travelling community – this particular 'Church'. And what is perhaps most pleasing and unexpected is the gratitude that pilgrims show for the tiny gesture of hospitality that we offer, by writing in our visitors' book comments such as: 'A place of heaven on earth!'

The practice of pilgrimage

Less than half the pilgrims who pass by are practising Christians, in the usual sense of that word, and even fewer previously knew of the Emmaus story. Many describe themselves as 'spiritual but not religious' – a topic to which we'll return in the next chapter. Few can articulate just what it is they are looking for in making the pilgrimage. Many seem to start as walkers and end up as pilgrims. I remember one young woman who only began to feel like a pilgrim as she started walking *back* from Santiago. And yet something draws them to undertake this ancient journey, living simply and with only a few necessities, towards the shrine of St James. They are searching for something that they do not find, or have not thought of looking for, in the Christian Church as it now exists. As they walk along this ancient path, sharing their stories or their hopes and disappointments with one another, they do not have to go along with any approved message or doctrine. Yet I do think that the Holy Spirit moves with remarkable freedom along the *Camino*, or perhaps I should say – because she is always and everywhere free – that pilgrims are especially open to her promptings.

What pilgrims do often find is support in their desolation and perplexities, the close and empathetic companionship of other pilgrims and sometimes of their hosts in the *gîtes* and *albergues*, which all echo what the two disciples walking the road to Emmaus experienced when they met up with the unrecognised risen Jesus. I particularly recall one pilgrim, who set out on the *Camino* as soon as he was released from a year in jail. He found himself making a real spiritual journey, supported and guided along the way by many others, including the monks of the beautiful abbey at Conques, where he had stayed for a week. Another pilgrim, who had set off from northern Germany and had already been walking for several months mostly sleeping out as he went along, had a similar story. He had decided during his walk to read the New Testament in order to be able to argue with his friends that it was all rubbish. But by the end he discovered he had become a believer, though he did not seem as yet to belong to any particular Church.

And whether they are sleeping in church porches or in graveyards – popular because they always have a water tap – or camping out in the countryside, or enjoying the relative luxury of a dormitory or B&B, pilgrims discover how little they really need by way of material possessions. A few even decide to practise extreme poverty, and undertake their pilgrimage without any money at all, choosing instead to rely on the generosity of others.[2] And, like poor people who have little, pilgrims are usually generous with what they do have – notably sharing their food or their favourite foot balms and medicines. Perhaps surprisingly, pilgrims, even lone women, feel safe on the *Camino*. They all experience the physical pain and exhilaration of getting up each morning and setting off again along the road, notwithstanding tired muscles, blisters or worse, and facing perhaps drenching rain or blazing sunshine. Compared with the rush and busyness of ordinary life, the slow pace of walking, brings them closer to the beauties and abundant diversity of God's Creation – whether it is the small flowers by the wayside or the vultures circling overhead. Even the mechanical repetitive act of walking sets the mind free for wonder and contemplation. Pilgrims often drop into some of the numerous churches along the Way and perhaps pray silently, light a candle or just sit for a moment in thought, feeling solidarity with the thousands of people who have passed there before or with those they are thinking of as they walk along.[3]

Stopping at churches is part of the ritual of walking the *Camino*. But the greatest ritual is to be found at journey's end, with the midday Pilgrim Mass which fills the cathedral at Santiago almost every day. On some days the huge incense burner, the *botafumeiro*, swings across the church from high up in the nave. This, it is said, was originally intended to disguise the smell of the newly arrived pilgrims. To this is added the ritual hugging of the statue of St James behind the altar, which can bring tears to the eyes of many pilgrims after their long ordeal.

And often at journey's end pilgrims discover something unexpected, though perhaps not what they thought they were looking for – new insights, perhaps, or some peace or reconciliation, or a new way of perceiving the world and their life. This is beautifully illustrated at the end of the fictional film *The Way*,[4] when at least two of the principal characters find, not that they are changed persons, but that they have a greater acceptance of who they are. As we discussed earlier, often God answers prayer, not by giving us what we ask for, but by showing us the situation or problem in a new light. The problem is not necessarily 'solved' but somehow it just disappears as a problem.

What strikes me most in my reflections on the *Camino* is that no one is in charge; there is no overall authority. Sure, the religious authorities in Santiago organise the Pilgrim Masses and the issuing of the certificate of accomplishment – the *Compostela* – to those pilgrims who wish to mark their achievement. And, sure, there are many organisations, such as the Confraternity of St James in the UK, which support and guide pilgrims. But they are not formally 'in charge'. So, although the *Camino* is undoubtedly Christian, it is not run by the Church, or any other institution. Rather, all along the Way it is the initiative of religious groups, local village congregations, even private individuals, and, of course, the pilgrims themselves, who mould the *Camino* into a Christian community.

Pope Francis has expressed the hope that the Church would cease to be a closed group of believers, but rather become a 'field-hospital' open to all in the daily struggles of life. The *Camino* offers a tentative model of what such a Church might be like: a mutually supportive community, without hierarchy, open to all comers, undogmatic, and witnessing to an alternative, less materialistic way of living life. It brings people together in their essential humanity, regardless of their status in 'ordinary' life or their nationality or ethnic background. What matters on the Camino is the daily physical challenges faced by each pilgrim, simply as a human person, the mutual support between them, and the discarding, for a time, of possessions superfluous to their immediate needs. So should be the Church.[5]

So, the *Camino* carries the marks of Jesus' teaching, and, in its own way, it demands something of his commitment, even if the perseverance needed by those who walk the Way is hardly to be compared with Jesus' dedication to what he knew from his Father, which led to his being tortured and murdered for it. At the same time a pilgrimage along the *Camino* also has its own rituals, which all religious communities need – the open 'sharing' with others, dropping into churches, leaving a stone at the *Cruz de Ferro*, or hugging the statue of St James in the cathedral at Santiago, and later receiving your *Compostela*.

Labyrinths

In earlier Christian times, for those who were unable to go on a pilgrimage, walking a labyrinth was considered to bring the same kind of spiritual benefits. A labyrinth should not be confused with a maze. A labyrinth has just one twisting path to the centre and back again and the route is never in doubt, whereas a maze offers alternatives and dead ends. People have been creating and walking labyrinths for thousands of years and across many different cultures. They appeal to something in the human psyche in our search for the Transcendent. In recent years there has been a revival of interest in this ancient form

The labyrinth in the author's garden

of prayer. The most famous Christian labyrinth can be found on the floor of Chartres Cathedral in France. But many other churches and cathedrals, have them; for instance, there is one on the floor at the entrance to Ely Cathedral in England.

We have a labyrinth in our garden at home. It is in the style of the one in Chartres Cathedral, but somewhat simplified. The twists and turns – sometimes approaching the centre sometimes moving away from it – can be seen as a metaphor for life or a spiritual journey. The path itself is of paving stones, set in rough grass. At the centre of our labyrinth, we have eschewed a specifically Christian symbol and have instead placed a standing stone – an ancient symbol for humanity's straining for the 'unknown' beyond ourselves.

In a traditional pilgrimage, before the days of modern travel, arriving at the pilgrimage destination was only half the journey;

you still had to walk back, though probably many never did reach home again for one reason or another. Similarly, with a labyrinth, the centre is the desired destination, where you can lay down your emotional and spiritual burdens before tracing the path out again. We tell labyrinth pilgrims that they may wish to leave something at the centre before taking the return path out – as a renewed person returning to the familiar world. One day I found someone had left a silver necklace hanging on the central stone. I have often wondered what journey, what life story, that necklace represented.

1   See http://caminoaccueilarthez.org/
2   Jesuits today are required, at some point in their long training, to make a pilgrimage without carrying any money.
3   In Spain, the churches are often richly decorated with gold leaf and pictures and statues; in France, with a different history, they are generally more austere – which is more to my taste.
4   *The Way*, 2010, directed by Emilio Estevez.
5   To some extent, I romanticise here! There is certainly a phenomenon of '*Camino* tourism', by those who just want to 'tick off' walking the *Camino* on their bucket list. This applies especially in the last hundred kilometres before Santiago – the minimum distance that has to be walked in order to qualify for a *Compostela*.

6 Spirituality

Many of us, whether we have any religious faith or not, have an experience, on one or more occasions in our life, that can really only be described as 'spiritual'.[1] For a brief moment we are overwhelmed by a sense of a benign presence, something quite out of normal experience. We may sense this through some place or through an activity that for us is life-giving – music, art, mathematics, social relationships, sex perhaps – or there may sometimes be nothing in particular that triggers the experience, which comes completely unexpectedly. We may be inclined to dismiss the occasion or attribute it to something we can understand – such as day-dreaming. Yet very often such an experience is held in our memory for the rest of our life and we may even identify it as a moment when our life changes in some fundamental way. On the whole we do not talk about such an occasion because it is almost taboo to do so, but also because we cannot find words to express it – at least, not words that would convey the depth of the experience to someone else.

Yet those of us who have this type of experience, while being generally hesitant to share it with others, may nevertheless feel comfortable to describe ourselves as 'spiritual'. Indeed, we are probably more comfortable in doing so than would have been the case, say, a hundred years ago, when the apparent certainties of science and religions were seen as irreconcilably opposed to each other and there was no space left between them for just being 'spiritual'. In our time, there is no taboo on being 'spiritual'. It almost seems that the decline in formal religious affiliation has accompanied a rising spiritual awareness.

'Spiritual but not religious'

Consequently, people often say something like: 'I'm spiritual, but not religious.' I suppose what they mean by the first part is that they certainly recognise the existence of a benign Other beyond themselves, and may find that they desire and can get in touch with this presence, at least to some degree, or even that this Other makes itself known to them.

How does this play out? What often seems to happen with this religion-less spirituality is that it actually calls people into goodness. 'Goodness' encompasses a huge range of possibilities – everything under the sun, indeed. Some, for example, go on pilgrimage, as we saw in the last chapter. Others are passionately committed to saving 'nature', the environment – looking after God's Creation – in different ways, ranging from disruptive protest and political action to practical permaculture farming.[2] Others might have a vocation to combat the arms trade or similar evils, or to work for the vulnerable and neglected in our very unequal society, others again just to love and care for those closest to them. From a Christian perspective, I sometimes observe such goodness – this sense of vocation that so many experience – and feel convinced that the Holy Spirit has escaped the Churches, where Christians so often seem to want to confine her, in order to work elsewhere![3]

The second part of the expression – 'but not religious' – implies that, for the person concerned, belonging to a particular religion would tie them down to a restrictive set of beliefs, practices and obligations that they don't want to submit to. This is a widespread view in society, and bearing in mind that the origin of the word 'religion' is the Latin *religio*, meaning 'an obligation' or 'a bond', the phrase 'tie down' hardly seems inappropriate. But this is odd. Jesus' teaching, and that of Paul and other New Testament authors, is not about being 'tied down' but rather about being 'set free'. Yet the popular perception of Christianity, at least viewed from outside the institutional Churches, is that membership actually does tie you down.

So, a major theme of this book is that adherence to the basic tenets of Christianity is not so much a 'tying down' as an invitation into *wonderment*. Philosophers, theologians and scientists continue to reason and research in the attempt to improve our understanding of ourselves and the world we live in, and they make great strides. But wonderment is the territory of mystery, where many of the questions about life and our nature as human beings remain unanswered and unanswerable, because, as Christians believe, wonderment is the place where we meet God. Although the beliefs of Christianity are often expressed in simplified or succinct ways, they are in reality a set of unfathomable mysteries that we can never fully understand or assent to. In one 'spiritual experience' in my life, not many years ago, all these mysteries, became absolutely and peacefully clear and comprehensible. But it was just for a brief moment and I could not possibly explain how this clarity came about.

For some reason, the mainstream Christian Churches, with their services, rituals and tired language, are failing to speak to those who just feel themselves to be spiritual.[4] It is as if the Churches are wary of such unfocused spirituality, perhaps because they have an existential fear that God might be acting outside their immediate control – like opening a Pandora's box that would then be impossible to close. Yet many of the most significant figures in Christian history actually experienced this sense of being touched by God and were quite open about having done so. We might think of John, the apostle and evangelist, Paul, Dionysius, Augustine, Bernard of Clairvaux, Aquinas, Dante, Thomas à Kempis, Meister Eckhart, Teresa of Ávila, John of the Cross, the anonymous author of *The Cloud of Unknowing*, Ignatius, Julian of Norwich, Teilhard de Chardin and of course many, many more.

Fortunately, alongside the formal institutional Churches, there exist many traditions of Christian spirituality – that is, particular ways of living out the mysteries of Jesus' teaching, different ways of approaching God. It is striking how many of these practices – silence, monastic life, pilgrimage, poverty and asceticism, for example – echo those of other great religions of the world. Once again, it is as if God draws people into mystery regardless of the particular set of formal beliefs from which they start. Because of the universality of these practices, it seems useful to summarise some of them in the Christian context.

Christian spiritual traditions and monasticism

The tradition of solitary prayer and meditation dates back to the early days of Christianity – Anthony the Great, also known as Anthony of Egypt, is the earliest known example. Towards the end of the third century, he went off to live and pray alone as a hermit in the Egyptian desert. Eventually, as so often seems to happen to hermits, a group of other would-be hermits gathered around him, and he established what is often considered to be the first Christian monastery.

Benedict was also initially a hermit, living in Italy in the sixth century, and, like Anthony, he went on to found communities of monks. The original Rule of St Benedict, in particular his guidance for abbots, who lead monastic communities, is a classic treatise on effective

The cloister in the abbey on Mont-St-Michel, Normandy

leadership, and is sometimes used in modern secular leadership courses and seminars. Benedictine spirituality animated the great abbeys of Europe in the Middle Ages, which were often at the heart of culture and civilisation in times of political turmoil. They were always built around an enclosed and covered cloister adjacent to the abbey church. Benedictine spirituality is encapsulated in the Latin phrase *Laborare est orare* ('To work is to pray'). The monks divided their time between *prayer* and chanting in their churches eight times each day and *work* – often on their vast farms, or in scriptoriums, where they painstakingly copied and illustrated the scriptures and sacred books before the invention of the printing press. The Benedictines are also dedicated to hospitality and to providing for the destitute. When I was 18 and hitchhiking through Europe with a friend, we arrived in Salzburg in Austria. We were hardly destitute, but we had nowhere to stay, so we knocked on the door of St Peter's Benedictine Abbey in the centre of the city and were offered hospitality for the night, with no questions asked or payment demanded.

Other monastic communities have their own rules and traditions. Among the strictest are the Carthusians, who spend most of their time in prayer in their individual cells and almost never receive visitors. The film *Into Great Silence* is a largely wordless documentary of the life of the Carthusian monastery at Grande Chartreuse, north of Grenoble, which is the 'motherhouse' of the order.[5] The German director Philp Gröning originally asked the monastery for permission to make the documentary in 1984. Sixteen years later he received an affirmative reply. Clearly time moves at a different pace for them than it does for most of us.

The friars ('brothers') of Franciscan spirituality are deeply committed to poverty. They follow the teaching of Francis of Assisi (d. 1226), who came from a wealthy family but turned his back on material possessions. Their spirituality is particularly open to God as revealed through Creation, and to working with the very poor.

Several of these religious 'congregations' also have female communities of religious sisters (nuns). I once knew a Franciscan sister who gave me a small stone as a symbol of Creation. I have treasured it ever since. She was Irish but worked in Nigeria, and spoke of the immense joy she found in going into Nigerian prisons and chatting and having fun with the prisoners. Such a vocation is way beyond my comprehension. Some congregations,

Benedictines and Franciscans in particular, also have a tradition of 'oblates', ordinary 'lay' Christians (those who are not priests or ministers) who do not become monks or nuns but who affiliate themselves with the congregation concerned and try to follow its spiritual tradition.

Finally, I will mention Julian of Norwich, who appears elsewhere in these pages. She was an anchorite in the fourteenth century. Anchorites were hermits of a sort, who had themselves walled up in a small cell for the rest of their lives – in Julian's case, against the walls of what is now St Julian's Church in Norwich. They were solitary but not isolated. Friends or servants would pass food and drink through a window, to which others would also come to seek spiritual advice or counselling from the anchorite, or perhaps sometimes just to chat! A second window opened into the adjacent church or cathedral, through which they could participate in the Mass or other religious services. Julian had a series of visions, or 'showings', of the Passion of Jesus, which she recorded in two books – the short and long versions of her *Revelations of Divine Love* – which have been a source of Christian inspiration ever since. I have known two people who died with her book on their bedside table. Julian is considered to be the first female writer in the English language.

Most of these congregations now have difficulty in attracting new members, at least in the West. But their spiritual traditions continue in other contexts. One example is the ecumenical monastery at Taizé in Burgundy, whose members come from several Christian denominations. Every year it welcomes tens of thousands of Christians, mostly young, who often camp in the grounds; the community has a world-famous practice of worship, exemplified by its

The meditation room at Bonnevaux

tradition of modern chant, and its life is centred on prayer, song, personal reflection and sharing. Another quite different example is the World Community for Christian Meditation (WCCM), which in the last few decades has revived the tradition of silent meditation. WCCM is largely a 'virtual' community that has now established a huge network of Christian meditation groups throughout the world. It is mostly organised and managed by lay people and, like Taizé, also cuts across Christian denominations. In 2020 I had the good fortune to visit the beautiful former abbey of Bonnevaux, just south of Poitiers in France, which is now the WCCM headquarters and a retreat centre, where people can stay for a period, engaging in the practice of silent meditation.

In so far as these different spiritual traditions all encourage a deeper relationship with God, we cannot say that one is better than another. Some people will respond to this spiritual tradition, others to that one, depending, perhaps, on their particular need or stage in life. And although most practising Christians do not consciously adhere to a specific spirituality, many follow practices that amount to an implicit spiritual tradition. For example, among Catholics, devotion to Mary, the mother of Jesus, is very common, and many routinely pray to God through the intermediary of Mary, or visit the various Marian shrines, such as that at Lourdes.

As noted earlier, the deeper someone is drawn into a particular spiritual practice, the closer they seem to move towards those coming from a different direction. At an inter-religious level, on 27 October 1986 Pope John Paul II organised in Assisi a World Day of Prayer for Peace, which was attended by no fewer than 160 leaders of Christian Churches and other religions; on that occasion, he, and they, were acknowledging a common belief in a transcendental Other whom many would call 'God'. So far as the Catholic Church is concerned, that such an event should take place at all was a remarkable confirmation of the teaching of the Second Vatican Council that God is at work in *all* the religions of the world. This teaching marks a radical and astonishing departure from the way the Catholic Church previously viewed itself, and was – often still is – viewed by others. But it also begs the question: 'Why then be a Christian at all?' To this I can only repeat the answer given in the opening paragraphs of this book: because Christianity, more than any other religion, tells a uniquely powerful story of God's love for and close relationship with the world in which we live.

Ignatian spirituality

My own experience and practice is of Ignatian spirituality. Ignatius (1491–1556) was a Basque from a minor noble family. He was a soldier but after being wounded in the battle of Pamplona in 1521 had a conversion experience. At the age of 33, he went to Paris to study theology, where he remained for more than ten years. During this period, he gathered around himself a small group of companions, whom he guided in prayer. Thus was born the Society of Jesus, more commonly known as the Jesuits. The Society expanded rapidly, many of its members, including Ignatius, were ordained as priests, but then dispersed as missionaries to distant corners of the world, including India and later China. Ignatius himself remained in Rome, leading the Society from there, and eventually publishing his *Spiritual Exercises,* in 1548.

The *Spiritual Exercises* are a distillation of Ignatius' own spiritual experiences throughout his life. It is not an inspirational book and should not be read as such, but rather is a manual for spiritual 'directors' taking other people through the discipline. Briefly, the Exercises are a series of meditations, intended to strengthen one's spiritual life – just as physical exercises are intended to strengthen one's physique. They are not a training in theology and do not require any deep theological knowledge or education on the part of the participant. They are always undertaken with an experienced spiritual guide, a spiritual director – like a physical trainer, I suppose – and usually, but not always, over the course of a silent retreat from the world for thirty days. The director, who is not necessarily a priest or pastor, must themselves have 'made' the Exercises at some point in their own life. Undertaken seriously, and with a good guide, they are an experience of being taken apart spiritually and psychologically and then put back together again, which very often is life-changing for the person concerned.

The Exercises are intended to be adaptable and flexible, but have an underlying logic and structure through several stages. We are first invited, through prayer and meditation, to contemplate and appreciate the gifts we have each been given in our life, and how these can be used to forward God's particular purpose for us. We are encouraged to adopt a principle of 'non-attachment', being willing to let go of anything that does not serve that purpose. This is not a general invitation to poverty or asceticism; it will depend on our particular situation and calling. From there we move on to contemplating God's love for each one of us and to self-examination of our failures and limitations, though not in a spirit of unconstructive guilt but rather in gratitude for God's forgiveness. The next section of the Exercises takes us through the life of Christ, starting with the Incarnation and going up to the end of his public ministry; these reflections are accompanied by a series of meditations on what is involved in committing our own lives to following Jesus, which ask us to consider or 'discern' any major 'life' decisions that we may be faced with at the time. The tone then changes from joy and fulfilment to one of sadness, as we take up the contemplation of Christ's Passion and death. This serves as a reminder that Jesus' promise is to be with us whatever our life brings, not a promise that we shall avoid suffering and disappointment. Finally, the experience of joy returns through focusing on Jesus' Resurrection and his subsequent appearances to his followers.

Presented in this way the Spiritual Exercises may not seem very profound. But they have to be experienced, entered into and lived in order to be fully understood. They can also appear to fall into the category of 'me and Jesus' spirituality. But that is far from the reality; they are purposeful and demand that we engage with the world in whatever way we are called to. Jesuits, whose lives are imbued with Ignatian spirituality, consider themselves as 'contemplatives in action', ever seeking new practical initiatives. There is, indeed, a joke that one of the three things that God does not know is what the Jesuits will do next.

A few final comments might be made about the Ignatian tradition. First, the *leitmotif* of this form of spirituality is 'finding God in all things'. Prayer and companionship with God are not separate from the rest of our lives. Second, there is a strong emphasis on 'discernment', which is a pattern of prayer and reflection, drawing on *all* our feelings, emotions and intellect, in order to find out what God wants for us and what he wants us to do. It is far more subtle, and indeed prayerful, than the simple but easily mistaken: 'God spoke to me and told me.' As I have stressed, God's actions and answers to prayer often come slowly and can easily be overlooked.[6] There is a beautiful image that God's desires are like water dropping on a sponge, whereas the desires and motivations of the 'evil spirit' (whatever we understand by that),[7] are like water splattering on a stone. Third, there is an Ignatian principle of the 'more'. The demands of the Exercises can seem impossibly hard to follow, but we *can* pray for 'more' – the desire to have the desire. Ultimately, God is in control and knows perfectly well that, of ourselves, we can never achieve the full commitment that seems to be demanded in the Exercises. There is always a possibility of 'more', which may or may not be offered to us. Indeed, not only can we not get *there* on our own, we cannot get *anywhere* without God.

Spirituality and religion

Let us return to the relationship between spirituality and religion. Generally, those who are 'spiritual but not religious' follow their spiritual practice or calling as individuals. But spirituality does not usually flourish in this way. We are sociable creatures: we need to belong to groups and communities. Prisoners in solitary confinement and all lonely people suffer mentally and spiritually from the loss of human company – as became very evident during the pandemic lockdowns of 2020 and 2021. So individual spirituality without community is not enough; it does not grow and deepen. Relationship is at the heart of who we are – just as it is at the centre of whatever the Trinitarian God is. People instinctively come together to celebrate and to pray. In the Christian tradition this implies belonging to one of the Christian Churches.

This raises the question: 'Even if I accept that my spirituality should be nurtured in some form of Christian community, why should I belong to a *Church*?' These days there is apparently no lack of alternative, organised communities, such as those already mentioned: the World Community for Christian Meditation, or Taizé, and many, many more, often smaller and more local. Three characteristics mark such gatherings: the groups often meet in someone's home, rather than in a church building; an ordained priest or minister is not required to be present as leader of the group; and the constitution of the group may cut across different Christian denominations. What the different participants may have in common is the shared practice of a particular form of spirituality – perhaps meditation, or devotion to the Franciscan, Benedictine or Ignatian traditions. Such groups offer the opportunity for Christian fellowship, but they are not Churches and make no claim to be so. Yet they draw their inspiration from the teachings of the Church, and usually their leadership from committed members of one or another Christian Church. In such gatherings the life of the Church is constantly being renewed and reinvigorated.

Yet the Churches themselves remain the bedrock of Christian community. Despite all their failings, they are the essential institutions and organisations that hold it all together, that provide structure to Christian worship and celebration, and in so doing provide inestimable support to the vast majority of practising Christians. Formally belonging to a Church, marked by the sacrament of Baptism, is such an integral part of the Christian life that in the next two chapters we shall consider how the Church – in the broad sense of that word, embracing all the Christian Churches together – came to be where it is today, along with the new challenges it faces.

1   Research carried out by David Hay and others suggests that this type of experience is widespread even among people who have no religious faith. See his *Religious Experience Today: Studying the Facts* (London: Mowbray, 1990).

2   Permaculture is an informal philosophy that might be described as treading lightly on the earth. It advocates farming going 'with' nature rather than 'against' it, using, for example, natural methods of pest control rather than manufactured chemicals. But the concept is broader than this: a whole way of life. See, for example, Graham Bell, *The Permaculture Way: Practical Steps to Create a Self-Sustaining World* (East Meon, Hampshire: Permanent Publications, 2004).

3   God certainly calls prophets from among non-believers. I doubt that Greta Thunberg would even remotely consider herself a prophet (though I don't know the state of her relationship with God), but she certainly has the right profile – an unimportant, marginalised person in the world, but someone who felt that she had no choice but to speak out regardless of where it would take her.

4   The various Charismatic movements within the Church may be something of an exception to this.

5   *Die Grosse Stille (Into Great Silence)*, 2005, directed by Philip Gröning.

6   On the other hand, God does not always act subtly. The apostle

Paul was thrown to the ground and struck blind on the road to Damascus (Acts 9:1–22). Presumably this was the only way for God to get the attention of a stubborn man, as Paul seems to have been!

7   I doubt the existence of a personified devil, but I do think that we are all open to the presence of evil – or, rather, the absence of God – an experience that can seem just as real and powerful as if evil were a living being.

Part III: Jesus' Teaching as Religion

The Christian Story is an odd one, because it is not fundamentally about being Christian but about being human. The story that we re-enact each year points us not towards some cosy future in which all Christians will be gathered together around Christ, but towards the Kingdom in which all of humanity will be reconciled and united. To be a Christian is to claim that one's ultimate identity is to be found only in unity with the whole of the rest of humanity.[1]

We have seen a few of the many ways in which we can build, maintain and deepen a personal one-to-one relationship with God, who is always present and available to all who seek to find him, and who is ever eager to reciprocate in love. Nevertheless, we are not individual, isolated persons. There is a dimension to becoming people of God that requires community. This usually means belonging to one of the Christian Churches, which sustain most Christians in their faith, but which are nevertheless human institutions subject to failure and now in need of renewal.

1   Radcliffe, op. cit., p. 2

7 The Life of the Church

For the vast majority of practising Christians, the Church of which they are members is the basis of their spiritual life and of their communal prayer, particularly through church services or 'liturgy' (formal prescribed religious practice). This is where they find their spiritual nourishment through a sense of community, or perhaps simply because this is where they feel they *belong*.

Worship and belonging

The services of different Churches display extraordinary diversity. At one end of the scale, people can be sustained by the very ritualistic and formal liturgy of the solemn Eucharistic services of the Catholic and Anglican Churches, which are essentially the same, and the Orthodox Church, where the form is very different. This liturgy might take place with a huge congregation in some great, ancient cathedral, whose magnificent architecture itself seems to invite contemplation of the Other beyond ourselves, whom we can never quite grasp. The sense of mystery may be enhanced by the flickering of lit candles, the smell of burning incense, the wearing of elaborate vestments by those who preside over the service, and the choreographed movements of those playing supporting roles at the altar, while accompanied by the singing or playing of some of the most sublime music ever written. Such services have their own drama. At a Catholic Mass or Anglican Eucharist, one or more prayers and Bible readings are followed by a sermon, and then the drama builds up to a climax when the presiding priest repeats the words of Consecration, the moment when the bread and wine on the altar are *transformed* or 'transubstantiated' into the body and blood of Jesus (as is believed in the Catholic Church) or blessed and made sacred as *representing* his body and blood (as in Protestant Churches).[1] It is difficult not to be moved by participation in such an event. At the other end of the scale we find the quiet service, where very little is said and even less sung, with plenty of time for silent meditation, and with just a two-minute homily that draws attention to the central truth of whatever Bible reading is chosen on that occasion. This is the form of service where I personally find myself more 'at home'.

In between lies a great range of possibilities. Services in the non-conformist Churches (the Baptist, Methodist and other Protestant Churches that do not 'conform' with the Church of England) can be very simple, with a judicious mixture of communal prayer, singing by the whole congregation, a reflective homily or sermon and possibly the distribution of communion. This simpler rhythm also offers ritual and is not lacking in its own drama and ceremony. In a different context, in the great Benedictine and similar monasteries, the monastic community comes together several times a day to pray and worship, through the chanting of the Psalms of the Old Testament to the almost hypnotic music of Gregorian plainsong. A few years ago I attended such a service during a wintry February weekend in the ancient abbey of Sainte-Foy at Conques, a village tucked away in a remote corner of southern France and seemingly still stuck in the Middle Ages. I then realised for the first time why a hood or cowl forms part of a monk's habit (or gown) – the church was freezing cold.

Whatever the form of particular church services, generally they are open, welcoming and accepting towards anyone who chooses to come. You can be lonely, confused, misguided and not very lovable, and church people will still accept you, give you a place and provide a framework for connection in a way that is harder to find outside the Church, particularly in the individualistic and fractured society in which we now live.

It is in these varied rituals and services that most Christians sustain and deepen their faith: this is where, through Bible readings and preaching, they develop their understanding of Jesus and his teaching; this is where they receive their spiritual nourishment, which then sustains them in their daily life with all its joys and tribulations; this is where they may find themselves challenged out of a complacent acceptance of the ordinary ways of the world. Still, it must be admitted that weekly church-going, together with the religious services that mark significant moments in life – birth, marriage and death – are all that most practising Christians want. Consequently, most members of Christian Churches meet one another only before, during and after a Sunday service, or on some other significant occasion, in their church building, which then frequently lies echoingly empty for the rest of the week.

Nevertheless, my own experience of the institution of the Church is that it is brim full of good people – ordinary church members who offer their time and energies to support other people in one way or another, as well as priests and religious sisters who give up so many of what are usually regarded as the rewards and comforts of life in order to commit themselves to selfless work for others. I am convinced that God is at work with and through all such committed individuals.

This conviction was strongly reinforced while I was making the Ignatian Spiritual Exercises. At one low point, after about a week, I started thinking: 'What if all this is just massive brainwashing?' I spent some time walking the hills and lanes around the retreat centre, trying to answer this question. In the end, no doubt under the influence of the Holy Spirit, what convinced me otherwise was the enormous simple *goodness* – I can think of no better word – of the people making up the community that I had temporarily joined, both the spiritual directors and the other retreatants. I realised that the doubts I had been having were coming from some 'evil spirit'. But I also learned that evil forces may be weaker than we usually suppose, which is not how they are usually portrayed in films and the media. If we push them away firmly they can disappear.

But there is something else here that I find particularly compelling. If one excludes ancient institutions, such as the Pharaonic civilisation of Egypt, of which we know little but which existed when time moved more slowly, the Church, despite its many internal divisions, is arguably the longest-surviving human institution, having been in existence now for 2000 years. It has been fragile at times and frequently pervaded with failure and evil. But what it has done over those twenty centuries is to keep the memory and teaching of Jesus alive and present in the consciousness and conscience of humankind, continuously bearing witness to the mystery of Jesus, the Word, who strongly identified with the poorest and most marginalised people in society and turned worldly wisdom upside-down. As we have repeatedly seen in these pages, every doctrine of the Church is a mysterious paradox beyond our normal understanding: a God who is remote and inconceivable but closer to each one of us than we are to ourselves; three persons in the one God; Jesus as God and man; the virgin birth; and not least the impossibility of the Incarnation and Resurrection, which taken together encompass the most important event in human history. The Church, the Catholic Church at least, has insisted that both sides of these paradoxes must be maintained: it is a mistake to deny either clause of the paradox. We cannot hold, for example, that Jesus is just God, or the opposite – that Jesus is only man. Rather, we hold to the mystery hidden in the paradox, because it is in the mystery that faith resides. Each one of us must live with and within that mystery, in whatever way we can manage, for that is where God is to be found. In the end, many of us remain practising Christians because, like Peter, we say: 'Lord, to whom can we go? You have the words of eternal life' (John 6:68).

Yet although the Church, all the Christian Churches, may be keeping Jesus' memory alive, the reality is that, at least in the West, Church membership is declining and younger people are no longer attracted to join. The Churches need to renew themselves. How this might be done is a theme of the rest of this book.

Eucharistic celebration

Let us go back to the beginning. My old schoolfriend Nicholas King spent ten years of his life writing a new translation of the Bible.[2] I remember asking him one day how he intended to translate the passage in the Gospel of Matthew where Jesus says that Peter is the 'rock' on which he will build his Church (Matthew 16:18). After a moment's thought, Nick answered:

'The word used in the Greek original is *ecclesia*, and that's usually translated as "Church".'

'But', I objected, 'Jesus never intended to start a Church. He can't have said that,' to which Nick replied:

'No! Jesus may not have said that, but Matthew did!'

My question reflected something that constantly strikes me in the Gospels. Throughout his life, Jesus seems mostly to have been concerned with how we should lead a *fulfilled* life, how to live our lives to the full as God desires for us; he was not trying to establish a new religion, or indeed a new form of Judaism, which was the religious context in which he lived. At the end of his life, he did not leave a blueprint or set of instructions for his disciples to follow after he had gone. Rather, in his long discourse at the Last Supper on the night before he was crucified, he expressed great confidence in his disciples by placing the future in their hands – while promising that the Holy Spirit would come to help them (John 14–17). Then, during the meal with his disciples, he blessed and broke bread, shared it out, and passed around the cup of wine, making the extraordinary and, indeed, troubling statement that the food and drink were his body and blood, and telling his companions to repeat this sharing in memory of him.

What emerged after the Resurrection, and particularly

after Pentecost, was the enormous energy of the disciples in spreading the 'Word' – the new message about the significance of Jesus' life, death and Resurrection – as Luke recounts in the New Testament book the Acts of the Apostles. Up to that point the disciples had always seemed somewhat confused and uncertain, but now they were confident and knew what their mission was. As a result of their teaching, the first followers of Jesus – both Jews and gentiles (those who were not Jews) – started to live together, sharing their possessions. Importantly they celebrated Jesus' memory by re-enacting his Last Supper in shared meals:

> They devoted themselves to the apostles' teaching and fellowship, to the breaking of bread and the prayers.... All who believed were together and had all things in common; they would sell their possessions and goods and distribute the proceeds to all, as any had need. Day by day, as they spent much time together in the temple, they broke bread at home and ate their food with glad and generous hearts. (Acts 2:42, 44–46)

It is worth remarking parenthetically that this brief passage is deceptively innocent. It not only disguises the radical and subversive character of what came to be the early Church, but also issues a challenge to our own understanding of 'Church' today. To the Jewish leaders and people, the early Christians were guilty of apostasy and worse in claiming that Jesus – whom they had condemned as a blasphemer and law-breaker – was the long-awaited Messiah. And according to the Greco-Roman world view, even the declaration that there was only one God was a daring innovation. But perhaps most subversive of all was that these infant Christian communities consisted of people from all strata of society, from aristocrats to slaves, rich and poor, women and men, Jews and non-Jews, as equals in

God's eyes. This had never happened before.[3] And we have to recognise that over the last 2000 years and in our own times, the Church has frequently fallen away from this egalitarian principle, which disregards race, gender, nationality, religion, wealth, social class and circumstances, just as it has often turned its back on the concept of responsibility for the material well-being of all God's people.

To return to the theme of the Eucharist, today in Churches of all denominations Eucharistic celebrations follow a formal prescribed ritual, a liturgy, that varies from one Church to another but is in most respects essentially the same. They have lost the convivial atmosphere of these first Christian re-enactments of Jesus' Last Supper. The model of Jesus' shared meal has become stylised to the individual administration of a small quantity of the consecrated bread and wine by the priest or an assistant to each worshipper.

During the period of COVID-19 lockdown, when normal church services were prohibited, such Sunday gatherings of Christian communities became impossible. Many priests celebrated the Eucharist online through Zoom or Facebook, enacting the ritual in splendid isolation in front of a computer. It was impossible for their congregations physically to receive the bread and wine; instead, people were invited to participate vicariously by means of a 'spiritual communion'. This, it was carefully and somewhat illogically explained, was not the 'real thing' but was as good as the 'real thing'; the reasoning was that God cannot be tied down to a particular ritual but can be present anywhere and in any context of God's choosing. This is certainly true, but this argument and the circumstances that gave rise to it should provoke the Churches to think more deeply and imaginatively than they have done in the past about how to experience the loving presence of God in the world *other than* just through regular Sunday services in church buildings yet while retaining the physicality of bread and wine.

Renewing the Eucharist

Personally, I have long dreamed that the Eucharist might again often be celebrated in the context of a shared meal, as it was in the very early years of the Church's existence. Groups of Christians could gather in someone's home, with a priest or minister, to pray together, to listen to some Bible readings and reflections, and then to re-enact what Jesus did at the Last Supper during a communal meal. Such Eucharistic celebrations already take place from time to time, but the first step of renewal would be to make this practice more frequent and widespread. Liturgies for such celebrations could become much more flexible and spontaneous, without omitting the crucial aspects of the Eucharistic liturgy: acknowledging our sinfulness and God's forgiveness; prayers and Bible readings; the Consecration and the sacramental sharing of the consecrated food and wine.

If such Eucharistic gatherings were to take place frequently, we would need many more priests than the Churches now have, and as the recruitment of full-time priests in such numbers is impractical from many points of view, another and different form of priesthood is needed instead. At the moment, the path to ordination as a priest in most Churches is long and demanding, usually requiring prior higher education and academic study. Ordained priests or ministers are then integrated into the administrative structure and hierarchy of their own Church. Some go on to ascend the hierarchy and become bishops or assume other high-ranking roles. A consequence of this is the emergence of clericalism – a clerical culture which seems to mark out priest and bishops as a special group,

Pilgrims beside the Sea of Galilea in Israel await the celebration of the Eucharist

different from everyone else. This has been a particular failing of the Catholic Church.[4]

A different form of priesthood could be much simpler. Those concerned – let us call them 'Eucharistic celebrants' – would be nominated by their own local Christian community, on the basis of their recognised faith, maturity and commitment. Then, after a short period of discernment and training, they would be licensed, or 'ordained', by their particular Church to preside *only* over small, sacramental Eucharists in their local community. They would have no formal place or responsibility in the administrative structure of their Church. Rather, their particular responsibility would be to ensure that the intimate celebrations of the Eucharist that I envisage here could be conducted legitimately, and that they would be open and welcoming to anyone who wished to come and participate. I am emphatically not proposing a kind of closed assembly for a particular social group – like a middle-class dinner party or a small clique of existing church members. Indeed, this form of 'Church outside the church' could be a way of bringing in the friends and neighbours of the central group; the friends might not be churchgoers, but might come, initially, for social reasons. They would not be constrained to 'sign up' to the faith.

One of Jesus' parables (Luke 14:15–24) seems to echo this idea. He talks of a great feast to which all the 'great and the good' were invited; but when the feast was ready all these guests made excuses to decline. In the end, the host ordered his servants to go and find people in the highways and byways – 'the poor, the crippled, the blind and the lame' – to come to the feast instead. If Christians did the same, I am convinced that slowly – for God works slowly – the Holy Spirit would breathe new life into the Christian communities at the local level, and from there would permeate society as a whole.[5]

A wonderful and speaking image of what happens when hospitality is offered to people who would not otherwise come together in this way is shown by the film *Babette's Feast*, even though it is not explicitly a religious allegory.[6] Babette, who is a famous Parisian chef, comes as an unknown refugee to live in a small Danish village, inhabited by strict, and frankly gloomy, Protestant Christians. For many years she works without wages as a humble servant for a pair of middle-aged sisters. One day she wins the lottery and uses all the proceeds to prepare a beautiful meal for the villagers, such as they have never before experienced, including wine. In the course of the meal her neighbours are transformed into a joyful, forgiving, loving community. The film is secular and Babette is not presented as a priest, but the story is frequently interpreted as a portrayal of the Eucharist. There is perhaps no human activity that draws people into community as deeply as the breaking of bread together. Jesus knew what he was about when he told his followers to make eating together the centrepiece of their communal lives – their 'Church'.

A wider approach

I have focused here on the communal celebration of the Eucharist, because that is the central ritual of the Christian community and Jesus clearly intended it to be so. But, across all the Churches, there are numerous small, informal initiatives of Christians coming together for prayer, or for meditation, or for studying and praying on the Bible and so on. Although many such initiatives are encouraged and supported by their local parish or Church community, I think a challenge for the institutional Churches is to acknowledge and embrace such initiatives, without domineering or dictating to them.

In a thought-provoking open letter to Pope Francis, Claire Henderson Davis, the daughter of Charles Davis, whom I mentioned in the Introduction, expresses a desire for new forms of priesthood. She argues that many of the post-Second Vatican Council generation of Catholics, who have left the Church, or 'who are hanging on by their fingertips', see the Church as: 'benignly irrelevant, if not actually detrimental to human flourishing'. She writes:

> Where are my generation, particularly in the West, looking for God? Not in church pews or homilies, or even in the Eucharist, but in practices like yoga, psychotherapy, and tribal rituals from other cultures that promise wholeness of body, mind and heart, offering an experience of intensity and transformation. I wonder if our imagining of priesthood can broaden to meet this need? Not dismissing the Church's existing sacramental priesthood, but making space for other ministries to be called priestly.[7]

She is certainly a voice crying in the wilderness, but a re-imagining of the Minor Orders, which still exist in the Catholic and Orthodox Churches, might enable the Church to sanction and legitimise the sort of roles that she imagines.[8]

Nevertheless, the traditional practice of celebrating the Eucharist in church buildings, often with large congregations, would still have an important place in the life of the Church and would not become redundant. There will always be a need for the wider Christian community to come together in worship and prayer, in churches, magnificent cathedrals and even outdoors, under the presidency of a priest ordained in the long-established way. Humanity needs to share and experience ritual and drama and solemnity. We still need to sing and hear the beautiful music that has been written and performed over the centuries as part of Christian worship. But we can retain the richness of the Church's liturgy and the functions of its formal organisation at the same time as instituting gatherings of local Christians for the intimate sharing of food in a communal meal, held in Jesus' memory, as he instructed his followers at his Last Supper or, indeed, in other simpler and perhaps novel ways.

1 Gallons of theological ink have been spent trying to explain what 'transubstantiation' actually means. But it is clear that for Catholics, Jesus is 'present' in the bread and wine after the consecration in some manner that goes beyond mere 'representation'.

2 Nicholas King (trans.), *The Bible: A study Bible freshly translated by Nicholas King* (Buxhall, Suffolk: Kevin Mayhew, 2013)

3 In a letter to *The Tablet*, 20 May 2020, Oliver Iglesia Victorio writes: 'what was natural morality in antiquity was the "assumption of inequality". It was the Christian moral revolution – where all humans bore the image of God and each individual had direct access to salvation – that gave European civilisation its distinctive morality.'

4 The development of such clerical roles has been accompanied and reinforced by special, and probably relatively recent, titles such as 'Father', 'Reverend' and 'Very Reverend', and not least 'His Holiness the Pope', as well as by particular forms of dress, such as soutanes and bishops' mitres.

5 During the 1960s in Latin America – Brazil especially – there arose a movement to establish Basic Christian Communities, similar to the model I suggest here. But they were not Eucharistic communities and were never fully integrated into the structure of the institutional Catholic Church, because the conservative hierarchy of the Vatican, including Pope John Paul II, unjustifiably saw them as suspect and Marxist.

6 *Babette's Feast* (in Danish), 1987, directed by Gabriel Axel. The film is based on a short story of the same title by Karen Blixen, published in 1958.

7 *The Tablet*, 11 April 2020

8 The Minor Orders were official, but non-clerical, roles within the Church, such as acolytes, exorcists, doorkeepers and readers, though it is no longer very clear what the precise duties of these Minor Orders were at any particular time in history.

8 The Church – A Way Forward?

The American scholar Raymond E. Brown points out in his book on the early Church that the very first Christian communities were geographically spread out and probably had little contact with one another.[1] Their structure was so minimal that they could hardly be called 'Churches'. But the new faith began spreading so rapidly that it was no longer viable for these small congregations to continue unconnected with each other and – human nature being what it is – they were at risk of straying away from the essence of Jesus' teaching. So around the end of the second century, these infant Christian groups began to coalesce into a recognisable institution – the Church.

From one Church to many Churches

Despite debates and disagreements, and the frequent suppression of teaching considered to be heretical, the Church, largely centred on Rome, endured for centuries. Initially it existed in the surroundings of a society that was essentially pagan. A landmark move came in AD 313, when the Roman emperor Constantine made Christianity the official religion of the empire. From that moment on, through the decline of the Roman Empire, the fluctuating fortunes of the Middle Ages, and right up to the period of the Enlightenment, the Church wielded political as well as spiritual power throughout essentially Christian territories that came to be called Christendom. Even now the Church is, or has recently been, too frequently associated with political regimes: the Catholic Church in Italy, Spain, Ireland and now Poland; the Orthodox Church in Russia; and the Anglican Church in England. This has led inevitably to moral compromise, though it may also have exercised restraint on unbridled political power. Notwithstanding spasmodic attempts to curb their absolute power, most rulers in Christendom for many centuries claimed to rule by 'divine right', thereby giving their rule legitimacy.

Subsequently, the Roman Church split into what has now become a considerable number of separate Christian Churches: first, the Eastern Orthodox Church split away in 1054, and then, in the sixteenth century, the German monk Martin Luther initiated the Reformation. His protest was based initially on theological objections, though it also touched on corruption and various scandals in the Roman Church. It set off a movement of reform and the eventual creation of a number of Protestant Churches. In both these cases, the breakdown of the hegemonic hold of the Roman Church was associated with – I do not say caused by – political changes: in the first case, the split of the Roman Empire into Western and Eastern empires, and, in the second case, the increasingly independent status of various Germanic states in what had come to be known as the Holy Roman Empire. The fissiparous nature of the Church continues, with the rise of numerous Pentecostal Churches of different kinds across the world.

In Christendom, up to the Reformation, belonging to the Church was taken for granted – albeit the Roman Church in the West and the Orthodox Church in the East. It was a fact of life, publicly acknowledged and supported, and was an important aspect of social cohesion, as witnessed by the presence of a church building in practically every village in Europe.[2] Indeed, Christianity was probably the glue that held society together. This is not to say that people were 'better' then than they are now; there is no evidence for that. But Christianity provided the shared stories and myths and the common customs – such as attending church every Sunday – that cultures and societies seem to need if they are to hold together.

Ostensibly, although the initial splits of the Reformation mostly concerned points of Christian doctrine and practice, the driving forces of division were also to do with power and politics, and not infrequently they even led to warfare. Eventually, for many and complex reasons, Western societies moved towards secularism, which is now, to a greater or lesser extent, their common basis. Whether people now choose to belong to any particular Church, or to another religion or to none at all, has become a purely *private* matter – entirely one of individual choice. Society is now governed and sustained by secular, non-religious, institutions and laws, rooted though these are in Christian and ultimately Jewish beliefs and norms.

This secularisation of society – in the west and increasingly throughout the world – poses a problem for the cohesion of the institutional Churches, particularly for the Catholic Church, which, with 1200 million members across the world, is by far the largest Christian Church. If adherence to a set of Christian beliefs to which everyone unquestioningly subscribes, a common observance and a certain hierarchical order are no longer the norm, what holds the Church together as a praying Christian community? The Catholic Church has yet fully to adapt to this trend. It is still very centralised around the Vatican in Rome, which tries to maintain some unity by requiring more or less blind obedience on the part of ordinary Church members to orders and instructions from the centre, which the laity, and to some extent the clergy, increasingly just ignore – not least when they concern questions of personal morality. In this sense it has indeed become a 'religion' in the original sense of that word – a tying down – and not a place of wonderment that it should be. The Catholic Church, as with all the Christian denominations to a greater or lesser extent, needs to transition to a new identity, a new way of being 'Church'.

Towards a new future

We should start by considering honestly what it is about the Church today that is off-putting to many ordinary people. In some denominations it may be the continuance of a clerical culture, which seems to set apart some Church members – the clergy – from the rest. To this we might add variously: too close an association with political power; apparently ostentatious wealth; insistence that members sign up to beliefs and creeds that may be difficult entirely to accept; and most recently the exposure of sexual abuse, within the Catholic Church particularly, but within other Churches also.[3] Although in some cases misguided, in others heinous, these are the failings of a flawed human institution, which, of course, is what the institutional Church is. We need to dig deeper.

I think that the most important factor is that the public voice of the Church is no longer loudly proclaiming the utterly radical and subversive nature of what Jesus taught and who he was. It often defaults instead to language, terminology and religious practices that no longer resonate with the lived experiences of most people. The Church teaches that Jesus 'saves'. But people are entitled to ask: 'saves us from what?' How does Jesus save us from abusive relationships, violence, poverty, homelessness, despair, discrimination, addiction, mental health issues? Here lies the challenge the Church now faces. The response to this challenge, the way forward, is a much more vigorous and open engagement with the myriad social and personal problems and distresses that afflict the whole human family, in a way that injects a specifically Christian perception of the world and all people, rooted in the controversial and radical teachings and life of Jesus himself. The Church, and all of us who are its members, need to find ways of living out this teaching as something fresh and new, rather than as something that has been in the background of our lives as the inheritance of 2000 years.

It will not be an easy path to follow. For a long time, we Catholics were used to the idea that the Church was quasi-perfect, directly under God's command. Indeed, the First

Vatican Council in 1869–70 decreed that the pope was 'infallible' – that is, incapable of error when teaching about faith or morals under very tightly defined conditions.[4] After that, the Catholic Church, or at least its members, suffered from a belief in 'creeping infallibility', an idea that since, on those strictly defined occasions, the pope was infallible, he must be correct on pretty much everything he says. In my youth, it would have been taken for granted that the Catholic Church was the only route to 'salvation', and that the end of the world – Jesus' Kingdom – would come when the whole of humanity had become Catholic! Thus, we solemnly prayed for the 'conversion of England'. Now I prefer to think that the world will end at the moment when these religious institutions are no longer needed and 'Christian community' takes on a new meaning – as adumbrated in the quotation at the head of this Part of the book.

From a personal perspective, I count myself fortunate that, in my teens in the early 1960s, I read a book by the Swiss theologian Hans Küng – it was probably *The Council and Reunion*, first published in English in 1961 – in which he laid out his view that the Church is not so much a sacred institution, especially favoured and directed by God himself, but a rather fallible human institution, subject to all the usual human failings.[5] Küng was writing just before the start of the Second Vatican Council (Vatican II, 1962–5), which breathed new life into the Catholic Church, or rather was receptive to the breath of the Holy Spirit. The doctrines and documents of the Council were enormously radical compared with what had gone before: they took the Catholic Church off the pedestal on which it had placed itself, and made it more open to God's work and his presence in everyone and in all religions. Sadly, over the last fifty years, much of the official Church hierarchy, all the way up to the popes, has resisted to a greater or lesser degree the 'breath of fresh air' that Vatican II blew through Catholicism.

Pope Francis

If Vatican II was one major turning point in the renewal of the Church, the election of Pope Francis in 2013 was another. Facing an uphill struggle against his many enemies in the Vatican itself and among many Catholics elsewhere, notably in the United States – where Catholics, being generally prosperous, have more resources than the poor to propagate their views – he is slowly but determinedly implementing change. He wants to focus on God's universal love for, and mercy towards, everyone. He is trying to move the Catholic Church away from its obsession with individual morality – for example, over sexual mores – to the more pressing issues of social injustice and existential threats in the world: poverty, slavery, exploitation and persecution, huge inequalities in wealth across the world and within societies, the continued existence of nuclear weapons, and the destruction of the fragile resources of our Sister Earth – God's beloved Creation. His encyclical letter *Laudato Si'* [*Praise be to You*]: *On care for our common home*, which was published in 2015 and addressed to all people in the world, pulled these issues together, not least because it is the poor and marginalised who are most harmed by environmental degradation.[6] More recently, in 2020, he published another encyclical, *Fratelli tutti* [*All brothers*]: *On fraternity and social friendship*, which focuses more particularly on the brotherhood and sisterhood of all people throughout the world.[7] It is again addressed to everyone and is, if anything, even more radically scathing than *Laudato Si'* of nationalist philosophies and obscene disparities in wealth, as well as the self-serving economic theories that now dominate most public discourse.

Further, there are signs of hope that Pope Francis is tentatively exploring the possibility of different forms of leadership and priesthood. In 2019 he organised an Amazonian Synod. This was a gathering in Rome of priests and lay people, especially representatives of the neglected indigenous peoples of the Amazon basin, to consider how the Catholic Church should move forward in that deprived region of the world. It was dominated by a debate over the shortage of priests, and discussion of the possible ordination of married men, (or *sotto voce* even women), to fill the depleted ranks of the priesthood. However, in Francis' summary of the proceedings, he ignored the debate over the ordination of married men, to the great disappointment of many of the participants and of many Catholics around the world, subsequently explaining that such decisions should be the outcome of collective prayer and reflection rather than of debate – the result of discernment in other words.[8] Instead he spoke rather vaguely of the need to find new forms of ministry that would be adapted to different circumstances and cultural traditions – both in the Amazon basin and elsewhere saying: 'efforts need to be made to configure ministry in such a way that it is at the service of a more frequent celebration of the Eucharist'.[9] This proposal is now being followed up in the countries of the Amazon basin. But whether the Church authorities, with or without Pope Francis, are ready to proceed as far as the proposals outlined in the previous chapter for frequent small Eucharistic and similar gatherings is very much more doubtful.

Still, the future development and growth of the Church will come from the margins, including the Amazon basin, and not from what used to be Christendom.[10] The Church needs to return, prayerfully and humbly, to the totality of Jesus' message – extreme and disruptive as it is – and ruthlessly eliminate from its teachings the accretions that have contaminated its doctrines and practices, starting with the ancient Greek philosophical underpinning, and continuing through the influences of misguided theology and political expediency right up to the present day. In different parts of the world, the Church should draw and build on what is good in local cultural traditions – even if this means sacrificing some superficial appearance of unity, which may, in fact, be no more than uniformity – just as in its early days it drew on the philosophical ideas and culture of the surrounding society in which it was first established. To give a few small examples: in many cultures dance is an important element in traditional spiritual practices, but it is almost entirely absent from the Western Christian tradition; many traditional communities feel strongly connected to their ancestors, which could be assimilated to the practice of some Western Christians of approaching God through the intermediary of the saints; and while the bread and wine of the Eucharist may have been the staple food and drink of Jesus' time and place, and of Christendom ever since, they are not staples in many other parts of the world, and could be substituted with other elements.

Francis' seemingly non-committal response to the debate about married priests at the Amazonian summit reflects his general approach. He does not usually confront his opponents directly with argument. He prefers to consider questions, whatever they are, from a different perspective and address them through discernment, rather than debate. Pope Francis is a Jesuit, and I perceive in his methods and actions the fruits of a long life imbued with the principles of Ignatian spirituality.

But discernment takes time. Notwithstanding the moves he has made, many in the Catholic Church think that Francis is being too cautious, too overpowered by the weight of conservatism within the Vatican, perhaps too fearful of the risk of schism. Women, in particular, are getting impatient with the slow pace of renewal. Most Christian Churches now ordain women to be priests or ministers. But the Catholic Church, along with the Orthodox Church, still does not permit this. Pope John Paul II actually decreed that the matter was no longer even to be discussed. But he was spitting in the wind. The question is increasingly debated among ordinary Catholics, who see the issue as purely one of unfair discrimination, and consider the theological arguments advanced against female ordination as baseless and self-serving. These arguments amount to making an antiquated distinction between men and women, where there is none. It is obvious to me that Catholic ordination should be open to women, and that one day it will happen.

Meanwhile, Pope Francis remains opposed to the ordination of women. This points to a major difficulty: the various proposals for reform and renewal require openness and rethinking in the official Church hierarchies, which, particularly in the Catholic Church, are notoriously conservative and rigid. In the end, I think it much more likely that the Holy Spirit will renew, or is already renewing, the life of the Church from the bottom up, from the initiatives and actions of ordinary practising Christians, and possibly in a multitude of largely unnoticed ways that are already happening – for example, in the varied initiatives that have sprung up along the Camino, as we saw in chapter 5.

A tradition of social action

Francis certainly wants the Church to engage more zealously with the existential issues of our time, to be more committed to social action in the world. In essence this would not actually be very new. What would be new would be this becoming a more distinctive sign of what being a Christian actually means – much more than just going to Church on a Sunday but publicly living the radical and counter-cultural teaching of Jesus. We shall explore some implications of this in the final part of this book. In the meantime, we should not forget the millions of ordinary Christians who do give their lives and talents to support others. One might think of a young lawyer who 'for the sake of the Gospel' chooses legal-aid work over a more lucrative practice; a doctor who regularly spends time in a war zone away from his clinic at home; church groups who take it in turns to staff a night shelter for the homeless and cook a meal every night; a Christian couple who foster damaged children; the Anna Chaplains who minister to the spiritual needs of isolated old people; Christians who take unpaid leave from their jobs in order to serve a stint caring for asylum seekers and refugees; Church networks that befriend lonely and housebound members of the community or run drop-in centres for dementia sufferers and their carers; those who give time and money to maintain and keep open their village churches for the benefit of the whole community (not just churchgoers); Church youth workers who provide safe environments and activities for young people who would otherwise have nowhere to meet and socialise; the volunteers who staff hospices, food banks, hospital driving schemes; and so on.

There is also a long tradition of communities of monks and religious sisters, such as the Benedictines and Franciscans, responding in a practical way to perceived social needs. In our own time, the congregation founded by Mother Teresa 'of Calcutta' is committed to caring for the dying and those forced to live on the streets. Most such religious 'congregations' are Catholic. They are less common in other Churches (at least as formal Church organisations), though it is noteworthy that the popular British TV series *Call the Midwife*, which is based on the memoirs of Jennifer Worth, revolves around an Anglican community of religious sisters working with poor mothers in the early twentieth century in the impoverished district of Poplar in east London – a typical calling for such Christian congregations.[11]

In recent decades, a noticeable trend has seen members of such religious communities move out of formal convents and monasteries and, in small groups of two or three, go and live among deprived people, where they devote their lives, say, to working with those who have been victims of slavery, or with children who exist by scavenging on rubbish tips. Others dedicate themselves to the needs of prisoners or refugees, or, on a larger canvas, campaign for reconciliation between warring groups. Usually, they work alongside other good and committed people of different religious affiliations or none at all (as *Call the*

Midwife illustrated).

In his, probably allegorical, description of the Last Judgement, Jesus says:

> Then the king will say to those at his right hand, 'Come, you that are blessed by my Father, inherit the kingdom prepared for you from the foundation of the world; for I was hungry and you gave me food, I was thirsty and you gave me something to drink, I was a stranger and you welcomed me, I was naked and you gave me clothing, I was sick and you took care of me, I was in prison and you visited me.' Then the righteous will answer him, 'Lord, when was it that we saw you hungry and gave you food, or thirsty and gave you something to drink? And when was it that we saw you a stranger and welcomed you, or naked and gave you clothing? And when was it that we saw you sick or in prison and visited you?' And the king will answer them, 'Truly I tell you, just as you did it to one of the least of these who are members of my family, you did it to me.' (Matthew 25:35–40)

I have no doubt that Jesus' generous invitation also extends to the numerous non-Christian people who do these things too, but, as we shall explore in the two final chapters, the Christian faith brings an intangible different dimension to such work.[12] Its subtle impact goes largely unacknowledged by the wider community. I am reminded again of Ignatius' image of water dropping on a sponge. As is sometimes said: 'Goodness does not make noise.'

So, I believe that in this century the most significant and vigorous sign of a continued Christian presence in the world is, and will be, found outside formal Church structures and buildings, but instead in the diverse activities of numerous Christians working for social and environmental justice either as individuals or as part of larger, Church-based or secular, organisations, charities and campaigns, and even political organisations.

1   This development of Christian Churches in the last third of the first century is described in Raymond E. Brown, *The Churches the Apostles Left Behind* (New York: Paulist Press, 1984).

2   At the same time, there were excluded groups, notably the Jews, who were at best tolerated but frequently persecuted in Christendom.

3   Enough has been written about the scandal of sexual abuse in the Church; I will not add to it here. Suffice it to say that one of the fundamental causes of this scandal has been the 'aura' of sacred power and a closed male clerical culture that the current concept of priesthood has generated. The proposals in this chapter would go some way directly to address this institutional 'cancer'. Nevertheless, I know of only one priest, among the hundreds I have encountered, who was convicted of such an offence.

4   This doctrine of papal infallibility has been used only once, by Pope Pius XII. As if trying out a new toy, in 1950 he proclaimed the doctrine of the Assumption, which states that Mary did not die but was 'assumed body and soul into heaven', as the doctrine is normally expressed. This may be true but it hardly seems fundamental.

5   Hans Küng, *Konzil und Wiedervereinigung* (Vienna, Freiburg and Basel, 1960), translated by Cecily Hastings as *The Council and Reunion*, translated by Cecily Hastings (London: Sheed and Ward, 1961)

6   *Laudato Si'* can be accessed or downloaded from the Vatican website at http://www.vatican.va/content/francesco/en/encyclicals/documents/papa-francesco_20150524_enciclica-laudato-si.html . It is discussed further in chapter 9.

7   *Fratelli tutti*, can be accessed or downloaded from the Vatican website at http://www.vatican.va/content/francesco/en/encyclicals/documents/papa-francesco_20201003_enciclica-fratelli-tutti.html .

8   *The Tablet*, 12 September 2020, p. 25

9   See   http://www.vatican.va/content/francesco/en/apost_exhortatio

ns/documents/papa-francesco_esortazione-ap_20200202_querida-amazonia.html , §86.

10 The word 'margins' is a bit of a misnomer. For example, in India there are believed to be nearly 24 million Christians – many more than in some nations of Christendom today. In China there may be more than 100 million Christians.

11 *Call the Midwife,* BBC period drama series, directed by Pippa Harris and Caro Newling. It started in 2012 and was still continuing in 2020.

12 Personally, I think that God's judgement must be like the way people often talk of the deceased at funerals – with nothing but praise for the goodness of the person concerned, as if their failings were of no importance. And why not? We are after all made in the image of God.

Part IV: Christianity in the World

In today's world, a few wealthy people possess more than all the rest of humanity. I will repeat this so that it makes us think: a few wealthy people, a small group, possess more than all the rest of humanity. This is pure statistics. This is an injustice that cries out to heaven![1]

We have established that there are two different dimensions to the relationship of human beings with God: the first is the two-way love of the individual and God for each other, and the second is the mutual support of Christians for one another in their quest for a communal and fulfilled life that is constantly guided by the Holy Spirit, and may be taken in surprising new directions. But the relationship God wants with us has a third dimension: the broken world in which God has placed us and where he wants us – alongside all good people who may or may not know God personally – to makes his presence felt through our love and service.

1   Pope Francis, General Audience, the Vatican, 26 August 2020, online at http://www.vatican.va/content/francesco/en/audiences/2020/doc uments/papa-francesco_20200826_udienza-generale.html.

9 The Transforming Work of Christianity

Jesus had several striking images to describe how his followers should interact with the rest of the world. He told them that they were the 'salt of the earth' (Matthew 5:13), and likened the activity of the Kingdom of God to that of yeast in a large measure of flour. Neither salt nor yeast is edible on its own, but both transform the food to which they are added, giving it flavour and texture. A third image is light: don't hide your light, Jesus says, but set it up to lighten everything it strikes. These three images suggest what the Christian presence in our deeply troubled world should be like – transforming it from within and shedding revealing light on it from without. In this final Part, I want to consider whether there is any specifically Christian understanding we can bring to bear on the state of the world, or any contribution that Christians can make that is not in conflict with the good work done by others, but alongside and in collaboration with them.

Faith, Hope and Love

In her series of online talks *A Living Hope: The Shape of Christian Virtue*, delivered in May 2020,[1] the Australian theologian Sarah Bachelard addressed these questions. As we saw in the first pages of this book, Jesus seems primarily to be concerned with human flourishing, but not in the sense of 'How to be happy', which might be the aim of a self-help primer, nor in the sense of 'How to get to heaven', which sadly has been the implicit goal of much Christian instruction. His teaching is altogether deeper than that. If we are all made in God's image, as the book of Genesis proclaims (Genesis 1:27), then the more we become fully human, the closer we come to our Creator God, until we reach a point where we become one with the Divine life itself. That is God's desire for us. As with much else in this book, the idea of being subsumed into God is mysterious, and an ultimate outcome of our search for him that we can never fully achieve. But, Bachelard argues, the three central characteristics of Christianity, that are normally referred to as 'virtues', are the means by which we make progress. Those virtues are Faith, Hope and Charity – or Love. (I capitalise these words because their meaning in this context is not quite the same as in common usage.) Ordinarily, a virtue is an aspect of good thinking and behaviour that we can nurture in ourselves and attain by our own efforts. Aristotle said, long before the time of Jesus, that the way to become a virtuous person is to practise virtue. Rather, Christianity teaches that Faith, Hope and Love are God-given gifts; they cannot be attained by our own efforts alone. Anyone who receives these virtues from God receives at the same time a particular responsibility.

Faith, Bachelard says, 'enables our trust in God's goodness'; without this what would be the point of an abstract, disengaged, belief in a loving God? Faith concerns our view of the world: is this ultimately a place of goodness, as Christians believe, or one irretrievably beset by evil? The answer will affect how we act in the world: 'Faith', says the theologian Paul Tillich, 'is the state of being ultimately concerned'.[2] The virtue of *Hope* 'enables us to forge, as Jesus did, a counter-story in the midst of the world's violence and in face of the temptations to despair'. It enables us to imagine new possibilities and to believe that God can bring them about. And *Love* or *Charity* 'is about seeing as God sees, seeing ourselves, seeing others, seeing everything whole'. To put it rather prosaically, these, simply stated but very fundamental, attributes are what Christianity 'brings to the party', as we collectively try to change the world. We have Faith in God's goodness, hold fast to the energising Hope that a better future is God's desire for the world and can be brought about, and commit ourselves to Love – to try to love as God loves every one of us and all of Creation.

The virtue of Faith is not about the details of what we believe; it is the ability to hold on to a belief in a loving God, and live out our belief joyfully in the presence of others.[3] This is not always easy. For example, nobody really knows why God permits suffering in the world: surely he could just fix it! He could, but he doesn't. Personally, I think that Love and suffering may be two sides of the same coin. When someone whom we love suffers, then we too suffer alongside them. So I wonder: since God is Love, does God also know suffering? He permitted Jesus – the Incarnation of himself in human form – to suffer violently, to the point of deep despair and death on the cross. Think about it for a moment. When Jesus in Gethsemane prayed in fear to his loving Abba, to find another way; and when he cried out from the cross 'My God, my God, why have you forsaken me?' (Matthew 27:46), do we really imagine God the Father sitting in heaven, or wherever he is, utterly indifferent to his beloved Son's pleas? I think not. I rather imagine the Father sharing deeply in that anguish, in that suffering, even though, for reasons that we cannot comprehend, he did not choose to put an end to the brutal murder of his Son that was taking place.[4] Ultimately, we do not understand why God allows certain things to happen, or does not intervene to prevent them. As scripture says:

> For my thoughts are not your thoughts,
> nor are your ways my ways, says the Lord.
> For as the heavens are higher than the earth,
> so are my ways higher than your ways
> and my thoughts than your thoughts. (Isaiah 55: 8–9)

Faith is the capacity to trust that, whatever happens, God is present in our lives, reaching out for us and wanting us to rely on him, whether we can see the way forward or not.

Hope goes beyond a blind optimism in the future. It can flourish even in the most 'hopeless' situations. Hope is an ability, in the teeth of all the evidence, to hold to a rival vision of the future, which is far more than some vague conviction that things are getting better and will turn out well, like a feel-good movie. Hope makes a narrative of what the future will be like and Faith enables us to believe that God will fulfil it. 'Hope … is not the belief that everything, was, is, or will be fine … [It] is an embrace of the unknown and unknowable, an alternative to the certainty of both optimists and pessimists.'[5] This is the kind of Hope that can flourish. Just as the physicist Carlo Rovelli earlier reminded us that 'reality is not what it seems', so the future will not be what we expect. At the present time, climate change and human inequality and exploitation are 'hopeless' problems in our world. In the case of the first, the measures agreed internationally and the actions individuals are encouraged to take are woefully inadequate to solve the problem. And in the case of the second, politicians trot out vague aspirations and so-called 'policies' without any real commitment to the radical, systemic reform needed to bring about the necessary changes, while 'trickle down' economics is a complacent argument that as the wealthy grow even wealthier the poor will benefit too – on the coat-tails of the rich, if you like – which may be true eventually, but at the cost of even greater inequality in income and wealth. Yet Faith proclaims that God will not abandon his Creation or his creatures, while Hope proclaims that the world *can* be righted and restored to health and beauty and balance. We may be able to conceive of what this looks like, but we don't know how it will happen.

The last thing Etty Hillesum, the Dutch Jewish diarist, wrote was a message of Hope written on a postcard that she addressed to her friend Christine, and pushed out of a crack in the side of the freight truck that was taking her to Auschwitz on 7 September, 1943. Against all the odds her postcard was picked up and posted by a local farmer. She wrote:

Opening the Bible at random I find this: 'The Lord is my High Tower.' I am sitting on my rucksack in the middle of a full freight car. Father, Mother and Mischa [her brother] are a few cars away. In the end the departure came without warning ... Goodbye for now from the four of us.[6]

Hope did not stop her from being murdered at Auschwitz two months later, just as the human person of Jesus, the Incarnation of God, was crucified, for reasons we don't understand. But in both cases what looked and felt like defeat was no such thing. Etty's life and her extraordinary writings have since inspired many people with Hope – a consequence she certainly did not expect.[7]

Charity, or Love, helps us to see others the way that God sees them, to radically proclaim the equality of all human persons as equally valuable and worthy of love, and to bear witness to that truth in the way we behave towards everyone we encounter, and to those we have the power to help, whether we meet them or not. God is also deeply in love with the whole of his Creation, with its beautiful abundance and exciting diversity. Both these themes were brought together in Pope Francis' encyclical letter *Laudato Si'*, in which he addresses not just Catholics but 'every person living on this planet' (§3).[8] His letter focuses on the impending environmental catastrophes faced by humanity and the earth together, and examines the issue of social injustice in the world; the two are closely interconnected.

Laudato Si'

Laudato Si' is a truly inspired and remarkable document, which has been, and should be, widely read by many people of all beliefs who are concerned with the issues facing our modern world. I commend it to you. It is so rich that it is difficult to summarise its ideas or to represent its content by quoting from it. Francis accepts the scientific consensus on climate change and other aspects of environmental destruction, and he endorses the various measures that we are told are essential if we are to overcome these existential threats. But research and policy and action, he says, often imply an *instrumental* view of the earth, as if it exists merely to satisfy human needs. Rather, we should see the earth as part of God's beloved Creation, valuable and lovable *in and for itself*, not just for our purposes. Indeed, the title *Laudato Si'* is taken from the first two words of a canticle of St Francis of Assisi, in which he addresses the earth as our Sister.

Pope Francis stresses that in the biblical narrative God found that *all* his Creation – not just humanity – was 'very good' (Genesis 1:31). So, when God gives humanity 'dominion' (Genesis 1:28) over the rest of Creation, he does not intend to grant us a free hand to do whatever we want with it, but rather calls us to care responsibly for the created world in a way that is consistent with God's purpose.

> This ['dominion'] implies a relationship of mutual responsibility between human beings and nature. Each community can take from the bounty of the earth whatever it needs for its subsistence, but it also has the duty to protect the earth and ensure its fruitfulness for coming generations. (§67)

Francis goes on: 'we are called to recognise that other living beings have a value of their own in God's eyes' (§69), and quotes approvingly the German bishops' teaching that 'we can speak of the priority of *being* over that of *being useful'* (§69). He continues to develop this theme with a number of lyrical scriptural examples and references, stressing that the whole of Creation – a deeper and more mysterious idea than just the 'environment' or 'nature' – is an expression of God's bounteous love.

However, *Laudato Si'* is about much more than the environment and God's love for all of Creation. Francis questions the whole ethos and system of values of modern society. He writes: 'If we acknowledge the value and fragility of nature and at the same time our God-given abilities, we can finally leave behind the modern myth of unlimited material progress' (§78). There is a connection between ecological damage and social injustice and inequality across the world. It is those of us who are wealthy who have caused the damage and who continue to exploit the resources of the earth, but it is the poor who suffer the consequences. God sees all human persons, without distinction, as equally valuable, equally lovable, and the virtue of Love helps us to do the same. Of course, many people and experts pay lip service to this radical – even revolutionary – idea, without really taking it to heart or signing up to its consequences. On this, Francis has a paragraph that is worth quoting at length:

> It needs to be said that, generally speaking, there is little in the way of clear awareness of the problems which especially affect the excluded. Yet they are the majority of the planet's population, billions of people. These days they are mentioned in international political and economic discussions, but one often has the impression that their problems are brought up as an afterthought, a question which gets added almost out of duty or in a tangential way, if not treated merely as collateral damage. Indeed, when all is said and done, they frequently remain at the bottom of the pile. This is partly due to the fact that many professionals, opinion makers, communications media and centres of power, being located in affluent urban areas, are far removed from the poor with little direct contact with their problems.... This lack of physical contact and encounter, encouraged at times by the disintegration of our cities, can lead to a numbing of conscience and to tendentious analyses which neglect parts of reality. At times this attitude exists side by side with a 'green' rhetoric. Today, however, we have to realise that a true ecological approach always

becomes a social approach; it must integrate questions of justice in debates on the environment, so as to hear *both the cry of earth and the cry of the poor*. (§49)

More recently Francis has summarised the whole approach of *Laudato Si'* in a typically blunt and hard-hitting statement (already quoted, in part, at the head of this chapter):

[The] symptoms of inequality reveal a social illness; it is a virus that comes from a sick economy. And we must say it simply: the economy is sick. It has become ill. It is the fruit of unequal economic growth – this is the illness: the fruit of unequal economic growth – that disregards fundamental human values. In today's world, a few wealthy people possess more than all the rest of humanity. I will repeat this so that it makes us think: a few wealthy people, a small group, possess more than all the rest of humanity. This is pure statistics. This is an injustice that cries out to heaven! At the same time, this economic model is indifferent to the damage inflicted on our common home. Care is not being taken of our common home. We are close to exceeding many limits of our wonderful planet, with serious and irreversible consequences: from the loss of biodiversity and climate change to rising sea levels and the destruction of the tropical forests. Social inequality and environmental degradation go together and have the same root (cf. Encyclical, *Laudato Si'*, 101): the sin of wanting to possess and wanting to dominate over one's brothers and sisters, of wanting to possess and dominate nature and God himself. But this is not the design for creation.

The god of greed

For anyone seriously seeking to save the earth and address the iniquity of poverty and deprivation, a critical question is: What does it mean to flourish as a human person? As we have seen, much of Jesus' teaching revolved around this question. Unfortunately, modern society, at least in public secular discourse, has tended to reduce the concept of human flourishing to the desire simply to 'have more'. If you are struggling to put food on the table for your children or do not know whether you will eat tomorrow, or where you will sleep tonight – which is the situation for a large minority of the world's population, even in supposedly affluent countries – this is a perfectly understandable and justifiable desire. Those who don't have enough for life's basic needs are perfectly entitled to want more. But for those of us who already have sufficient, among whom I include myself and probably most people who will read this book, the idea that 'having more' is inherently good, that it is the key to human fulfilment, is simply absurd. Those of us in such a fortunate position should know that, in reality, there is much more to life than that. Sadly, many of us discover this only when some unexpected development in our life – such as the social restrictions arising from the COVID-19 pandemic – forces us to reassess our values.[9]

In the meantime, many political objectives, and the structure of our economies, revolve around this desire to 'have more'. Public policy is overwhelmingly directed towards the goal of perpetual economic growth. Another way of looking at this is that modern society has taken the ancient vice of greed, and turned it into a virtue. We may think of greed, or perhaps more strictly of avarice, as being 'miserly', Scrooge-like. But it is more subtle than that and so deeply embedded in modern culture and economic policy that we no longer notice it. We are so imbued with this way of thinking that we are largely unaware of it, just as a fish does not know it is swimming in water. The avaricious desire to have more is a false god worshipped by modern society. It may, even, comprise the shared panoply of beliefs and myths that hold our present Western society together – if indeed anything does – just as Christianity held Christendom together for more than a thousand years. And, as with all false gods and idols, it demands sacrifice. In this case, we offer it the sacrifice of the poor – all those who do not, *in fact*, have enough. We sacrifice the marginal and disregarded people of our societies, those who are economically useless and the 'undeserving poor'. We insist on buying cheap products – from food, to clothes, to electronic gadgets – disregarding the reality that low prices are often the result of slave or near-slave labour.[10] And we sacrifice the earth itself, which is mined and despoiled for its resources, which are then transformed into the pollutants that destroy it.

Yet, when you think about it, the main objective of our politics is really odd – outrageous, in fact. A society that already enjoys material abundance, with plenty of 'stuff' to go round for everybody (even though not everybody gets a sufficient share), has been persuaded by a corrupt political discourse to believe in the banal – indeed, pernicious – aim of acquiring more and better stuff, more fun, more excitement and more experiences; it is the culture of *consumerism*. Why do we fall for this, when we know that getting and having material possessions and ticking off adventures on our 'bucket list' may give us a brief thrill, but then leaves us feeling dissatisfied and unfulfilled? As has been said: 'Consumer culture perpetuates itself ... precisely because it succeeds so well at failure.'[11] If we really want to change this, if we want to let go of 'the modern myth of unlimited material progress', in Pope Francis' words, then we, in the prosperous world especially, will have to live without economic growth. Yet the political and practical problems of doing so, of moving from where we are now to a society that slays the god of greed are so formidable, so apparently unachievable, that the project just seems like idealistic 'pie in the sky'. It seems impossible to imagine our way out. In short, we need Hope.

The role of the Christian
You don't have to be a Christian to accept and act on this

analysis of the problems faced by our world; most thinking and campaigning around these ideas is being done by good people who may have no religious belief at all. The Christian contribution to the myriad problems faced by our world is not to come up with *different* solutions from those arrived at by other good, serious and knowledgeable people. Inevitably there will be disputes and compromises. Like everyone else, some Christians will hold one view on the way forward, others will hold another one. And nobody can work on all fronts at the same time: some will be 'called' one way, others a different way. Sometimes it will be right to protest, to go to jail even, sometimes to accept a compromise. There are no panaceas on offer. The Christian contribution is, rather, to transform our collective understanding of these problems, and their solutions, from the inside, from a different perspective, as we live out Faith, Hope and Love in our daily lives. It is to have the Faith that the one true God imagines a better world, in which everyone is equally worthy of respect and consideration. It is to have the Hope to trust that, ultimately, idols and false gods do not survive and that they will be defeated – probably in ways that we cannot imagine. And it is to have Love, which enables us to look on everyone in the world, and Creation itself, as equally valuable and loved. The Christian contribution, which may sometimes feel almost intangible, is not just to have a different *perspective*, but to do things in a *different spirit*.

There is no place here for self-aggrandisement. We, as Christians, engaging with others, should not adopt the attitude that *we* are going to show *them* a better way, how to do things differently. It is *who* and *what* we are that will make the difference, as with salt, yeast and light. In whatever we are called to do, we should approach our fellow humans in a spirit of service, listening empathetically to them and then responding to their felt needs and priorities, rather than imposing our own ideas of what's needed.[12] A Jesuit working with gang members in Los Angeles was asked: 'Do you guide them towards God?' He replied: 'No, they show me the way to God.' This answer inverts our usual understanding of the flow of help to the poor: we assume that the helper confers the benefit on the recipient. But the Jesuit found that, in his 'contact with the poor and the most excluded', it was he who learned about 'values and what is important in life'.[13]

All four Gospels describe the Last Supper. Three of them recount Jesus breaking bread and distributing it with wine to his disciples – the institution of the Eucharist. But the Gospel of John ignores this and tells a different story. Before the meal Jesus washed the feet of his disciples, a ritual that would normally be carried out by a slave or servant. Peter wished to refuse, but Jesus insisted. Afterwards he said: 'I have set you an example, that you should do as I have done to you' (John 13:15). In another place he says to his disciples: 'whoever wishes to be great among you must be your servant, and whoever wishes to be first among you must be your slave' (Matthew 20:26–7). These deeds and words are truly radical; they amount to a complete overturning of prevailing human wisdom concerning how we should organise power and status in society.

We should not expect to be praised or even acknowledged for making a difference. As often as not, we shall not even know that we are doing so. Among the many whose lives have expressed this, we might think of Dietrich Bonhoeffer, a German Protestant priest, who actively sought to overthrow the Nazi regime in Germany in the 1940s, for which he was eventually executed. In prison he wrote a beautiful poem: 'Who Am I?'. It reflects on the apparent strength he conveyed to his prison warders in contrast with the desolation he felt within himself. He did not know what difference his life had made or would make, yet he went to his death holding onto a Christian vision of a remade world. He had the faith to believe that it would be created, the hope that human desire would be directed away from false gods (in his case, Nazism), and the spirit of humble service in relationship that enacts God's love for each individual as uniquely valuable. All of these are what Jesus taught and what two millennia later we still need, and will continue to need, to learn until the final fulfilment of his Kingdom at the end of time.

Sometimes I wonder how Jesus himself, in his human nature, felt as he went about his task. Did *he* know he was making a difference? Or did he just carry on teaching and explaining, as his beloved Abba wanted him to, and living the person he was? Of course, *we* know the end of the story – Resurrection and everything that has followed from that. There are scriptural texts that suggest Jesus also knew that he would rise again on the third day, but these might be *post hoc* 'predictions' by the authors of the Gospels. It does seem to me at least possible that, as Jesus was led on his way to crucifixion, he had a deep sense of personal failure. But, at the same time, he knew with absolute confidence that God, his Abba, will not abandon the world that he created and loves, even if like us, in his humanity Jesus did not know how this would come about.

1   These quotes from the fourth lecture in the series Sarah Bachelard, *A Living Hope: the shape of Christian virtue* (2020), available at https:// www.youtube.com/watch?v=J6M86vnbwMU . The entire series has inspired much of this chapter.

2   Paul Tillich, *Dynamics of Faith* (New York: Harper & Row, 1957), p. 1

3   Jesus did not say: 'believe in the Apostles Creed', which was only formulated long after his departure from the world. What he did say was: 'believe in *me*'.

4   I suggested this thought at the funeral of my granddaughter, Isobel, in the hope that it might bring some comfort to her parents and relatives in their grief (see chapter 3).

5   Rebecca Solnit, *Hope in the Dark: untold histories, wild possibilities* (London: Canongate Canons, 2016), quoted in *The Tablet*, 15 August 2020, p. 27

6　Hillesum, op. cit., p. 426

7　Parts of her writings I cannot read aloud because they always bring tears to my eyes.

8　Quotations from *Laudato Si'* are referenced by their paragraph numbers.

9　There is a saying that nobody on their deathbed wishes they had spent more time in the office – that is, had spent more of their life earning the wherewithal to 'have more'!

10　Grace Forest, a co-founder of Walk Free, a foundation that is dedicated to eradicating slavery, writes: 'There is a high likelihood that the clothing, food and electronics we buy have passed through a supply chain rife with slavery and exploitation' (*Financial Times*, 23 December 2020).

11　Quoted in Tim Jackson, *Prosperity without Growth: economics for a finite planet* (London: Earthscan, 2009), p. 100, and attributed to Grant McCracken, *Culture and Consumption* (Bloomington and Indianapolis: Indiana University Press, 1990), chapter 7.

12　I once read an example of this. A charity was working to help impoverished farmers in Mozambique by providing them with agricultural tools. Further listening showed that what they really wanted was clothes to wear, as they could not go into their fields half-naked.

13　See https://jesc.eu/franck-janin-sj-on-the-jesuits-on-the-occasion-of-the-50th-anniversary-of-the-sjes/

10 What should *I* do?

As we come towards the end of this journey – descending from the mysterious, incomprehensible truths about God, and God's love for and presence in the world, down to the myriad problems that our world faces today – you may be asking: 'Well, what should *I* do?'

Some principles

Before considering this question, I should first offer a caveat. We need to recognise that many people in the world are in no position to *do* anything at all. Their lives are totally committed to looking after their immediate loved ones and family, or simply to surviving from one day to the next. But those of us who live comfortably in the affluent West – however complicated and over-committed our lives may be – can still make behavioural choices: for example, to travel by train or bus (or cycle) whenever possible; to turn down the central heating and instead wear an extra jumper; not to buy new clothes or gadgets just because the ones we already have are no longer fashionable; not to replace things that are broken, but rather try to repair them; to eat chicken rather than beef, the most environmentally damaging form of meat; not to buy products wrapped in plastic, which is then thrown away, and so on.[1] Most important for us all is to endeavour to treat everyone with whom we come into contact with respect and dignity, recognising that they too are images of the Divine Creator and are individually precious to God – in short, in the spirit of Love to try to see other people as God sees them.

By contrast if you *are* privileged to have the time, energy and resources to make a small difference in the world, I suggest two guiding principles. The first is to consider carefully where you should devote your time and energy; none of us can do everything.

There may well be things we think we *ought* to be doing, perhaps even accompanied by some sense of guilt that we are not doing them. But this is not necessarily the most reliable guide. You should pay careful attention to what you find yourself *drawn* into doing, perhaps quite naturally – even if this feels insignificant, irrational or even just too easy! What suggests itself to you may be something you can do in a way that no one else can – because of opportunity or because of your particular gifts or qualifications. Sometimes, however, you may have to dig deep into your basic desires, into what is 'life-giving' for you, with an openness to the quiet interior promptings that you experience. Such promptings usually come, as I believe, from God, but if that belief is a step too far for you, think of them as coming from the unknown Other, who is the source of life within you. A practice of meditation may help to open up this awareness. The reality is that many of our best and firmest decisions are made not just from the head but as much from the heart, or the 'gut'. By contrast, if you focus too much on what you think, or are told by other people, that you *ought* to do, then your decision is likely to be more superficial and fragile. We all have different talents, different roles to play and different contributions to make.[2] Quite possibly you will find that, after making a first tentative step in your chosen direction, you are taken into unexpected and wonderful places, and drawn into doing 'more', precisely because this is indeed God's purpose for you. Let me illustrate this idea with an example from Jesus' well-known parable of the Good Samaritan (Luke 10:29–35). The priest and Levite who passed by the injured man on the road no doubt had good, very rational, reasons for doing so, perhaps relating to ritual cleanliness or perhaps because they had a deadline to meet. The Samaritan, by contrast, had no good reason to get involved with an Israelite, one of the bitter enemies of his own people, so this was not something he 'ought' to do. But he was spontaneously 'moved with pity'; he was drawn to help the injured man and acted on this impulse.

Second, we are not going to change the world. That is God's work. All we are called to do is to be instrumental in some small way or another. At one point in his book *A Jesuit Guide to (Almost) Everything*, James Martin recounts how one day he explained to David, his spiritual director, his failure to persuade two friends to be reconciled with each other, and his consequent frustration. He said: 'Well, that's what Jesus would do. Jesus would help them to reconcile. Jesus would get them to talk to each other. Jesus would work until there was peace between them, right?' To this the reply came back: 'That's right. Jesus would probably be able to do all of that. But I have news for you, Jim. You're not Jesus.'[3]

In fact, I believe it is useful sometimes to think of the things Jesus did *not* do during his earthly life. We hear in the Gospels many stories of his healing the sick and consoling people in their suffering. But he did not engage in political activism, even though he lived in a society that was ruled and oppressed by the Roman Empire. No doubt, in his journeyings, he came across many unjust atrocities – people being crucified by the side of the road, cheated by the collectors of taxes for the Roman authorities, suffering religious persecution – but there is no record that he acted to remedy these wrongs. Jesus was not called to change his world by overthrowing the Roman Empire and establishing an alternative earthly kingdom of justice and peace. Indeed, during his forty days in the desert at the beginning of his public life he specifically rejected the temptation to do precisely this:

Then the devil led him up and showed him in an instant all the kingdoms of the world. And the devil said to him, 'To you I will give their glory and all this authority; for it has been given over to me, and I give it to anyone I please. If you, then, will worship me, it will all be yours.' Jesus answered him, 'It is written, "Worship the Lord your God, and serve only him."' (Luke 4:5–8)

God's way is manifestly different from the ways of the world. We have to 'trust in the slow work of God' – to refer again to the prayer attributed to Teilhard de Chardin. The human person of Jesus was limited by the time and place in which he lived, as we are by our own time and place. Yet, as the Incarnation of God, Jesus lives on in the world in many different ways, and his work continues, through the life and commitment of each of us.

Making a small difference

Few of us will be remembered in 2000 years' time.[4] Yet we all have a role to play in whatever is God's plan for Creation, though, even for the most important or saintly of us, that role will be miniscule, when seen in the context of God's dream for the world. It is said that Thomas Aquinas, the greatest theologian of all time, had a vision in 1273, in which he saw his lifetime's writing – 8 to 10 million words – as mere straw. After that he never wrote another word and he died a few months later.

In the previous chapter, I pointed out that our world faces two overwhelming issues: environmental destruction and social injustice. They are closely interlinked, as Pope Francis stresses in *Laudato Si'*. Both stem from a lack of Love, a refusal to see as God sees (in so far as it is possible for us humans to do that), to perceive and enjoy the beauty of Creation, and to acknowledge all our fellow humans as made in God's image and infinitely loved. Many of the specific good works that people do are related to one or other of these overarching problems. Thus, on the one side, some engage in protecting the declining number of insects in the

The Greenpeace ship, Rainbow Warrior, moored in London opposite Canary Wharf

world or fish in the sea, farm organically, or join in protest with Greenpeace or Extinction Rebellion, all of which are concerned with acknowledging and protecting the beauty and diversity of Creation. On the other side, some may campaign against the scandal of homelessness in our rich societies, the pervading and continuing existence of racism, or other forms of discrimination, or help to alleviate poverty, slavery and injustice in their own communities or in parts of the world far distant from their own, all of which are concerned with regarding and treating all human beings as equally worthy and lovable.

Some will say: 'I may not *do* very much, but I give money to charity.' That's okay; all these various activities need financial resources to support their work. But just giving away small sums can easily become a pretext for not engaging personally with the problems of our world or a salve for our consciences. Moreover, choose carefully. Some 'charities' actually lack 'Charity'. Giving money to people in need can be patronising, implying that those with the resources are more worthy than those who lack them. So far as possible, donate to those charities and organisations that work *with* those they support rather than just *for* them. Some charities are very concerned to be financially accountable to those who support them, while neglecting their social accountability to those whom they intend to benefit. This is an example of the phenomenon we noted in the previous chapter – the goal of financial efficiency and 'value for money' that has become such an overwhelming criterion in our society that we scarcely notice any more the distortion it creates in our attitudes. Moreover, the very rich people who give money to charity can easily come to think that their money and generosity give them the power and the right to dictate how their donations are used, and to influence the policy of the organisation concerned, or indeed to influence public and economic policy more generally. The unequal distribution of wealth is a cancer affecting our societies. The power that it confers on a small minority increasingly undermines many political and other social institutions that have been carefully nurtured over the generations. We have an expression: 'as rich as Croesus'. In fact, the very wealthy in our world are far richer than Croesus ever was.[5]

Destroying the god of greed

All small local actions have a place in the larger picture, which I now come back to as a way of finishing this discussion. Environmental destruction occurs and has occurred because richer people – that is *most* of us Westerners and not merely those who have accumulated obscene levels of personal wealth – have over-exploited the resources of the earth in order to satisfy our rapacious desire to have more. I have already observed that the only way to overcome this is to abandon the shibboleth of continued economic growth. When we – that is, those of us who already have enough, even 'plenty' – come to demand less 'stuff' and fewer 'experiences', then the earth will be better able to sustain us. Once the basic necessities of life, food and shelter particularly, have been attained for everybody, then other non-material things become rather more important for human flourishing – security, education, good health if possible, family and loving relationships. After a certain point, more stuff is simply not necessary. In *How Much Is Enough? The Love of Money, and the Case for the Good Life*, Robert and Edward Skidelsky point out that our current economic theories and policies are based on situations of *shortage*, whereas in the West we now live in economies of *abundance* – as, indeed, the title of their book (a father/son collaboration) implies.[6]

It is important to stress again here that, because of the pervading social injustice in our world, most people – many of those living in poverty in Africa, Asia, Latin America, but also the poor and marginalised in all corners of the world – still do not have 'enough'. They are entitled to enjoy the fruits and benefits of 'having more', at least to the point where they have the necessities to lead a fulfilled life. But these people are *not* those who have contributed to the environmental destruction of the earth. They may live surrounded by environmental destruction, such as deforestation or land laid waste by mining, but this destruction always occurs to satisfy the rapacious desires of those wealthier than they are. So the analysis presented in the rest of this chapter does not apply to those still living in poverty.

It will not be easy to destroy the god of greed, or straightforward to move away from our wasteful, throwaway habits, or from a society and economy that are overwhelmingly driven by 'having more', to something new and different and sustainable. Whole sectors, such as advertising, business and much of the financial sector, depend on engendering discontent by peddling the idea that having more stuff and diverse experiences is inherently good – that it is the key to human fulfilment. One consequence is the tendency to express almost everything – the beauty of a landscape, the advantages of getting married, even the value of human life – directly or indirectly in terms of money. The Harvard philosopher Michael Sandel has said: 'We drifted from *having* a market economy to *being* a market society.'[7]

There are two interlinked issues here. The first is that economic growth is a social treadmill. In order to keep the treadmill turning – to keep the economy growing – it is necessary continually to create new desires in us all. Much economic activity is directed towards stimulating these new desires. We are encouraged to want things that are strictly unnecessary, and which we did not even know we wanted before they were put before us. Ultimately, such activities have little or no socially useful purpose, other than to keep the productive economy running. Of course, many of those doing such jobs tell themselves that there is some purpose in what they do. How else, otherwise, could they look at themselves in the mirror each morning? Others, perhaps the thousands of people employed in call-centres reciting scripts to persuade someone to buy something they don't need, know that what they do at work is neither interesting nor socially useful. But they say: 'I have no choice; I have a family to support.' The real irony and scandal is that many of these 'bullshit jobs', as David Graeber vividly called them, are much better paid than the jobs that *do* serve a social purpose, such as caring for the elderly or the disabled, or nursing, or cleaning hospitals.[8] Cleaning public toilets may be a dirty, low-status, badly paid job. But it is not a 'bullshit job'. It does have a valuable, if not usually a valued, function.

This points to the second issue. Almost all 'things' and most 'services' – whether necessary or superfluous – are manufactured, distributed and delivered directly as a result of *paid* work. There are exceptions of course. People who do not, or do not any longer, engage in paid work – the unemployed, disabled and sick – are, usually barely, supported by the paid work of those in employment through their taxes, while most retirement pensions have been largely 'earned' through *previous* paid work. But the general rule is: if you want to benefit from what our economies have to offer, then you have to engage in paid work. To have income you have to be employed, and, in order to maintain 'full employment', it is necessary to stimulate the desire to have more stuff or experiences and then to satisfy that desire by manufacturing more stuff or inventing new experiences. This is what keeps the treadmill of economic growth turning.

However, the reality is that much, if not most, 'work' in the world is *unpaid*, and moreover is frequently done by women: caring for children and elderly relatives, keeping house and the daily task of preparing food. Unpaid work does not enter into the economic statistics. Hence, to boost the economic statistics, women are often encouraged to enter into the paid economy and then to pay someone else to take on their 'caring' role, even when this does not seem the most sensible or loving choice for their own well-being or that of the ones they care for.

So we seem to face an impossible dilemma. We appear to be dependent on continued economic growth and on maintaining a high level of paid employment in order to survive. But this same economic growth is destroying the environment – God's Creation. How then to slay the god of greed? The first step has to be to change the way we think about life and *what life is for*. Those who try to live simply, 'to *be* more rather than to *have* more',[9] are showing the way – how to be more open and available to other people and to the beauty and abundance of the world around us, rather than trying to take more from the resources of the earth.

As for the organisation of economic activity, a fundamental 'paradigm shift' will be necessary. Skidelsky and Skidelsky argue, as I do, that the shibboleth of economic-growth-at-any-cost has to be abandoned. They arrive at the conclusion that part of this paradigm shift would be to introduce a universal basic income (UBI) paid unconditionally to everyone in a particular society. Here is not the place to write a thesis on UBI; much has already been written on this topic and several partial experiments in UBI have taken, and are taking, place.[10] But the bare bones of the idea can be summarised as follows. The UBI in a particular economy might initially be set at a level barely sufficient to live on. Those who wanted to engage in paid work could, and would, still do so. For others, perhaps those with particular 'caring' responsibilities, a UBI might shift their marginal decision as to whether or not to engage in the paid economy. But ultimately the importance of the idea is that it breaks the link, hitherto taken for granted, between paid employment and the enjoyment of the goods and services that an economy of abundance has to offer.[11]

The usual, repeated, objection to UBI is that it would be unaffordable; tax revenue would be insufficient to pay for it.

Yet we have only to look around Western societies to see the abundance we already have. The underlying and scandalous problem is the unequal way in which this abundance is now shared out. Fundamentally, this is not an economic problem. It is, rather, the result of entrenched obstructiveness on the part of those of us who have enough, and our refusal to entertain a more egalitarian view of economic and social structures.

A similar paradigm shift that may be necessary, though one that so far is less discussed, concerns the way we think about private property. At the moment there is a universal assumption that people are entitled to as much wealth as they can legitimately acquire. But that assumption should be questioned. The commandment 'You shall not steal' (Exodus 20:15) is not a categorical prohibition. Many theologians would argue that the destitute are morally entitled to take (or 'steal') from the surplus of the wealthy. It is time to implement this radical insight – preferably of course by means that are recognised by law – to reduce the disparity between the poor of the world and those who have excessive wealth.

God's work, in which we can participate, is to change the minds and hearts of us all to turn away from the *status quo* to the *status Dei*. It is possible to hope for a different future. Whether or not UBI, or rethinking the assumption of an unlimited right to private property, become part of this future is unimportant in this present discussion; they are tools but certainly not panaceas. Poverty will never be completely wiped out; one way or another the poor and the marginalised will always be with us. But we can be confident that one day the god of greed *will* be destroyed, for false gods do not survive. We do not know *how* this will happen and, despite our best efforts to change the world, there may be much unnecessary human suffering before it does, not least as a consequence of active opposition, or just indifference, among those of us who currently enjoy wealth and power in our societies.

Nevertheless, Hope offers a vision of humanity slowly evolving to become more Faith-ful, more coherent, more compassionate and Loving. But, in the meantime, other idols and false gods will certainly arise. For we know that human society will reach full perfection only at the final coming of Jesus' promised Kingdom, at the end of what humankind experiences as 'time'.

And *our* future?

We have now journeyed a long way: from initially drawing from the well of life – which we call God – to practical and controversial proposals for economic change. It might seem like a journey from the sublime to the mundane, but much of Jesus' message was precisely about how human persons can flourish and become fully what God desires for them. Jesus did not propose specific social, political or economic theories, but he did illustrate his teaching with mundane, earthy parables from his own time and society, overturning conventional thinking and mores. In our own age and circumstances, we have to work out the details for ourselves, drawing on the three virtues: *Faith* that the unknowable Other is overwhelmingly in love with each of us; *Hope* that the goodness of the Other will eventually prevail, probably in ways that are quite unexpected; and *Love* that sees every person as precious and highly valued, and Creation as provided for us to admire, enjoy and use, but not to exploit and degrade.

We all have a part to play in the drama of human life. Yet our individual role and God's dream for the world and for humanity remain opaque to us. Many have probed, meditated on and written about this mysterious dream. Julian, the priest who married my wife and me in Botswana, discovered in his desert meditations that he was just scratching the surface. Ignatius in the Spiritual Exercises stresses that there is always *more* to discover, always the possibility of a deeper relationship with God. Aquinas came to see his enormous lifetime's work as straw. My own contribution, in this short text, is infinitesimally small.

After our death, although we may be remembered for a short while by our family and descendants, the world will eventually forget us all. Yet God will not. We shall rest, along with our loved ones, in the eternal present, and presence, of God's incomprehensible love. Jesus said:

Come to me, all you that are weary and are carrying heavy burdens, and I will give you rest. Take my yoke upon you and learn from me; for I am gentle and humble of heart, and you will find rest for your souls. For my yoke is easy, and my burden is light. (Matthew 11:28–30)

And Paul, reflecting on Jesus' life and teaching, wrote, with both wonder and delight:

Who will separate us from the love of Christ? Will hardship, or distress, or persecution, or famine, or nakedness, or peril, or sword? No, in all these things we are more than conquerors through him who loved us. For I am convinced that neither death nor life, nor angels, nor rulers, nor things present, nor things to come, nor powers, nor height, nor depth, nor anything else in all creation, will be able to separate us from the love of God in Christ Jesus our Lord. (Romans 8:35, 37–9)

Let us take Hope from this and again from Julian of Norwich's beautiful aphorism:

All shall be well, and all shall be well, and all manner of thing shall be well.[12]

1 A kilogram of beef requires an energy input around twenty times that of a kilogram of chicken. Since this energy frequently comes from grain, beef production requires far more land and energy to be used for growing grain. See David JC MacKay, *Sustainable Energy without the Hot Air* (Cambridge: UIT Cambridge, 2009) pp. 77–8.

2 These ideas come from Ignatian spirituality, which places particular attention to decision-making through 'discernment'. Ignatius stresses that all our important decisions should be made prayerfully and with our whole selves and personalities. We need to listen as much to our heart, our emotions and feelings as to what comes from our head.

3 Martin, op. cit., p. 258

4 Two Americans you may never have heard of are among the most likely to be remembered. They are Alan Hale and Thomas Bop, amateur astronomers, who in 1995 were the first to discover a new comet – designated the Hale-Bop comet – with an estimated periodicity of 2533 years. So around AD 4500 people may gaze at the sky and say: 'Look here comes the Hale-Bop comet again'!

5 Pope Francis explores these themes in his encyclical *Fratelli tutti*.

6 Robert Skidelsky and Edward Skidelsky, *How Much Is Enough? The Love of Money, and the Case for the Good Life* (London: Penguin Books, 2012)

7 Michael Sandel, *What Money Can't Buy: the moral limits of markets* (London: Allen Lane, 2012), p. 10

8 David Graeber, *Bullshit Jobs: a theory* (London: Simon & Schuster, 2018)

9 A slogan from CAFOD, the overseas development NGO of the Catholic Church in England and Wales.

10 It is not difficult to find literature on the topic, but one of the best short summaries was written by John Lanchester in the *London Review of Books*, 18 July 2019, which includes a bibliography.

11 In his book *Let Us Dream: The path to a better future* (London: Simon Schuster, 2020) Pope Francis also mentions the idea of UBI, p. 132.

12 Julian of Norwich, op. cit., p. 103

Credits

Etty Hillesum (detail from photo). Photographer: B. Meylink, 1937–1938. Collection Jewish Historical Museum, Amsterdam. All other pictures: © the author.

'Disclosure' and 'Moving Mountains' from *Watching for the Kingfisher* by Ann Lewin is © Ann Lewin 2009. Published by Canterbury Press. Used by permission: rights@hymsam.co.uk.

Front cover: a Byzantine mural in one of the cave churches in Cappadocia in Turkey. It has been partially defaced probably by the iconoclasts of the eighth century.

THE NEW OPEN SPACES

Throughout the two thousand years of Christian tradition there
have been, and still are, groups and individuals that exist in
the margins and upon the edge of faith. But in Christianity's
contrapuntal history it has often been these outcasts and
pioneers that have forged contemporary orthodoxy out
of former radicalism as belief evolves to engage with and
encompass the ever-changing social and scientific realities. Real
faith lies not in the comfortable certainties of the Orthodox,
but somewhere in a half-glimpsed hinterland on the dirt track
to Emmaus, where the Death of God meets the Resurrection,
where the supernatural Christ meets the historical Jesus,
and where the revolution liberates both the oppressed and
the oppressors.
Welcome to Christian Alternative... a space at the edge where
the light shines through.
If you have enjoyed this book, why not tell other readers by
posting a review on your preferred book site.

Recent bestsellers from Christian Alternative are:

Bread Not Stones
The Autobiography of An Eventful Life
Una Kroll
The spiritual autobiography of a truly remarkable woman
and a history of the struggle for ordination in the Church of
England.
Paperback: 978-1-78279-804-0 ebook: 978-1-78279-805-7

The Quaker Way
A Rediscovery
Rex Ambler
Although fairly well known, Quakerism is not well understood.
The purpose of this book is to explain how Quakerism works as
a spiritual practice.
Paperback: 978-1-78099-657-8 ebook: 978-1-78099-658-5

Blue Sky God
The Evolution of Science and Christianity
Don MacGregor
Quantum consciousness, morphic fields and blue-sky
thinking about God and Jesus the Christ.
Paperback: 978-1-84694-937-1 ebook: 978-1-84694-938-8

Celtic Wheel of the Year
Tess Ward
An original and inspiring selection of prayers combining
Christian and Celtic Pagan traditions, and interweaving their
calendars into a single pattern of prayer for every morning
and night of the year.
Paperback: 978-1-90504-795-6

Christian Atheist
Belonging without Believing
Brian Mountford
Christian Atheists don't believe in God but miss him: especially
the transcendent beauty of his music, language, ethics, and
community.
Paperback: 978-1-84694-439-0 ebook: 978-1-84694-929-6

Compassion Or Apocalypse?
A Comprehensible Guide to the Thoughts of René Girard
James Warren
How René Girard changes the way we think about God and the
Bible, and its relevance for our apocalypse-threatened world.
Paperback: 978-1-78279-073-0 ebook: 978-1-78279-072-3

Diary Of A Gay Priest
The Tightrope Walker
Rev. Dr. Malcolm Johnson
Full of anecdotes and amusing stories, but the Church is still a
dangerous place for a gay priest.
Paperback: 978-1-78279-002-0 ebook: 978-1-78099-999-9

Do You Need God?
Exploring Different Paths to Spirituality Even For Atheists
Rory J.Q. Barnes
An unbiased guide to the building blocks of spiritual belief.
Paperback: 978-1-78279-380-9 ebook: 978-1-78279-379-3

Readers of ebooks can buy or view any of these bestsellers by clicking on the live link in the title. Most titles are published in paperback and as an ebook. Paperbacks are available in traditional bookshops. Both print and ebook formats are available online.

Find more titles and sign up to our readers' newsletter at
http://www.johnhuntpublishing.com/christianity
Follow us on Facebook at
https://www.facebook.com/ChristianAlternative